Pat Robertson: A Biography

Pat
Robertson:
A BIOGRAPHY

by Neil Eskelin

HUNTINGTON HOUSE, INC.

Shreveport • Lafayette
Louisiana

Library of Congress Catalog Card Number 87-88020
ISBN Number 0-910311-47-1

Huntington House, Inc.
Lafayette, Louisiana

Typography and cover design by Publications Technologies
Printed in the United States of America

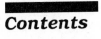

Contents

Acknowledgments

The research and writing of the life of Pat Robertson was enriched by many people whose contribution to the process made it possible.

To those outstanding individuals who shared their memories of Pat as a youth in Lexington, Virginia, I am grateful. These include Charles Glasgow, Julia Lewis Martin, Matt Paxton, editor of the *Lexington News and Gazette,* and Dr. William Pressly, former headmaster of the McCallie School in Chattanooga, Tennessee. I am especially indebted to George Lauderdale, Wilbur Presson, Bill Garthwaite and Henry Harrison for recalling their stories of the early days of CBN.

My thanks is also extended to the research librarians at the Virginia Military Institute, Washington and Lee University, the Sergeant Memorial Room of the Norfolk Public Library, University of North Carolina, Charlotte, and CBN University. And I thank my wife, Anne, for her advice and encouragement.

Finally, my heartfelt thanks is given to Rob Kerby of Publications Technologies, Melbourne, Florida, for his editorial expertise in the preparation of this book.

Preface

This book has been 25 years in the making.

As Pat Robertson's first full-time employee at his makeshift television station in Portsmouth, Virginia, one of my assignments in August 1961 was to prepare a promotional piece for WYAH-TV, which was about to begin broadcasting. With a borrowed typewriter, a pair of scissors, and some rubber cement, I finished the layout and took it to a little print shop.

"This is a piece of history," I thought, when I saw the first copy. And immediately, I began a file called, "CBN." That file has grown, and so has the man whose name is so closely linked with it — Pat Robertson.

When I was asked by a publisher to write this volume, my mind raced over the memories of the man I had worked with and had closely observed since that time. But what about the Robertson I did not know?

What forces and experiences shaped his early years? What about his parents? And why has he decided to enter the uncertain world of politics? Perhaps no individual on the current scene will be subjected to the intense light of scrutiny as Robertson. And that is because he is judged by a different standard. It is a religious standard. That's why even a minor character flaw or error in judgment becomes a major news story. Pat, because he speaks on moral issues, carries the expectation of perfection that goes along with it. Robertson, however, has not led a perfect life, and this book reflects that fact. He was a hard-drinking, fast-living college boy, and has no difficulty talking about it. But his friends do. For example, one of his fraternity brothers, who refused to be quoted on the record, told me, "Look. Pat and I did some wild things together. He can talk about it because that is the 'old Pat.' That was before his religious experience." Then he added, "But I still live that way. If I talk about those things, I'm really talking about the present. I haven't changed."

Without exception, the people I talked with had a deep respect for Robertson. Some expressed disagreements with his methods, his style, and even his philosophy — but they still admired Pat.

In my own case, resigning from CBN was one of the most difficult moments of my life. I walked into his office and began to cry as I told him of my decision. It wasn't as though I was leaving CBN, I was leaving Robertson. And he was bigger than life. He was a cause, a vision, and a "call" wrapped up into a powerful presence. It was more than a man I felt I was leaving.

When I finished this manuscript, I was asked, "Has this experience changed your opinion of Robertson?" Without question, it has. Even at the time I worked closely with him, I had no real idea of the depth of his decision to build a television network designed to impact the values of Americans. It was years later that I learned of the seven days he spent in an empty church in the slums of Brooklyn — armed only with a Bible and seven cans of fruit juice — before making his monumental decision.

And before writing this book, I did not truly understand the profound influence of Pat's mother and father on what he is today. Finally, I must confess, I was rather passive on the idea of Pat Robertson seeking the highest elective office in the land when I began actively writing this volume. In fact, when I first heard the idea, I laughed at the thought. But the deeper I looked, the more impressed I became. And as I finally compared his preparation, his experience, his commitment, his leadership, and his positions on issues, I could find no potential leader who even came close.

I did not write this book to promote the candidacy of

Robertson. I wrote it because I felt the full story of this unique American would be an inspiration to many — especially young people making decisions about their future. But in the process, I have become a believer, not just in Robertson, but in what he stands for.

Neil Eskelin
Charlotte, North Carolina

1

"Americans for Robertson"

What happened in Michigan on Tuesday, May 27, 1986, was called "the year's hottest political feature story" by *People* magazine.

Almost instantly, Pat Robertson faced dozens of photographers, TV cameramen and journalists. He was the number-one news story on Wednesday and had so many requests for media interviews that his staff quit counting.

It was billed as a head-to-head battle between U.S. Congressman Jack Kemp and Vice President George Bush. But the first round of Michigan's several-step delegate selection process for the Republican Convention of 1988 had an unexpected winner. Robertson ("Pat who?") had scored the political *coup* of the year.

Was the host of *The 700 Club* serious about a bid for the presidency of the United States? Could a Christian broadcaster, who had never held a political office, be a credible candidate? Were his supporters committed to him or just trying to show the world what the evangelicals could do at the polls?

The Freedom Council — a Robertson-backed organization — claimed over 4,500 candidates of a record 10,110 residents who qualified to run as delegates for step two on August 5, 1986. As one reporter observed, "That left Bush and Kemp trying to figure out who came in second."

It was a bitter blow for the Vice President. Michigan was the state where Bush had beaten Reagan by a large margin leading up to the convention of 1980. It was his friends who tried to give him an early boost for 1988 by scheduling the unusually early test in 1986.

Said Marlin Fitzwater, Bush's press secretary, who later became President Reagan's press secretary, "Just as a political fact of life, the Robertson showing has to be considered important."

The definition of news is "novel." The press had a heyday with Robertson.

Under headlines such as, "Are You Running With Me, Jesus?" "Pat Robertson Seeks a Lower Office," "The Wacko Factor," and "Heaven Only Knows," Pat was the target of satire, sarcasm and painful scrutiny — enough to make most men run for cover.

But not Robertson.

Certainly not his supporters who were now clearly behind his possible candidacy.

While Michigan's step one was a blow to Bush, step two was a seeming disaster for Robertson. When the August 5 vote was in, the same *People* magazine was saying Pat "finished either a well-beaten second or a distant third, according to differing accounts of the balloting."

What went wrong? How could the delegate selection process take such a curious turn?

Was it because potential delegates were not bound to a particular candidate that no one knew for sure who they would support? Or had the media decided to declare their own winner, George Bush, and paint Robertson as a backslider?

From August 1986 to February 1987 there was a noticeable silence on the part of the press regarding Robertson. With the exception of an occasional blurb regarding Pat's "testing the political waters" seeking signatures of support, he was a non-player. In fact, there were dozens of national stories reviewing major presidential hopefuls that failed to even mention the name of Pat Robertson.

Then, in a story that broke in the *New York Times* on Sunday, February 15, 1987, the real story of Michigan emerged. "Strategists for Vice President Bush," the story stated, "acknowledging that they overestimated their candidate's strength, now concede that … Pat Robertson won nearly as many delegates as the vice president in the state's precinct voting last August."

In fact, Robertson won more delegates than Bush, notes David Walters, the chairman of Michigan Committee for Freedom

"In Michigan with 52.8 percent of his delegates present," said Walters, "Robertson forces led a coalition of conservatives to the February state convention, took control of 12 of 18 congressional districts and elected a majority of members to the state central committee — which is the governing body of the Michigan Republican Party."

Said Peter Secchia, vice chairman of the Republican National Committee for the Midwest, who heads the Bush organization in Michigan, "It's a close race now, sure. The problem is that we designed a campaign to defeat (Robert) Dole, Kemp and (Howard) Baker and along came this new wave of activists." They, of course, were for Robertson.

Robertson had the smile of a winner when he said of his Michigan victory, "This is a very positive step for us. It looks as if we'll have 50 percent of the delegates at the state convention. You can draw your own conclusion, but to me it's pretty startling."

Make that "astonishing," says Walters. "Something Robertson's critics said would never occur has happened.

"His support has grown beyond an evangelical Christian base to include traditional conservatives within the party, Catholics and Orthodox Jews. This coalition nationally very well could give Pat Robertson the nomination in 1988.

"More significantly, his appeal to and support of charismatic Christians, fundamentalists and blacks, who have traditionally voted for Democrats in general elections, will play a key role in sending Pat Robertson to the White House in 1988."

Then, in March 1987 in South Carolina, the home state and familiar political battlefield of Vice President Bush's campaign manager, Robertson supporters upset the Bush strategy and elected a majority of precinct delegates, making Pat Robertson the frontrunner among party activists in that key southern state.

"Those victories," says Walters, "signify that supporters of Pat Robertson are working within the party to obtain the delegates required to capture the nomination for their candidate in 1988.

"The strength of Robertson's organization and its ability to win in major statewide conventions has broadened his appeal among many rank and file Republicans.

"It is interesting to note that Michigan in January 1988 will be the first state to select national delegates. South Carolina leads the pack among southern states by holding its primary on March 5, three days prior to the South's 'Super Tuesday' multi-state presidential primary election on March 8."

Pat Robertson.

Who is this surprise candidate, this dark horse who seems ready to take the Republican Party by storm?

"He is a statesman, not a politician. And I believe the country is ready for a statesman," says Marlene Elwell, 1984 Michigan field director for the re-election of President Reagan.

Robertson is a law school graduate. An economist. A successful businessman. An author on the *New York Times'* bestsellers list. The founder of one of the largest commercial cable television systems — CBN. The founder of a university. A familiar face in millions of homes every day on *The 700 Club.* The son of the late U.S. Senator A. Willis Robertson of Virginia.

But when did Pat begin to feel the pull of politics? And why would he set his sights on the nation's highest office?

"I've laughingly said, 'Right after I learned to say "Mommy" and "Daddy," I learned to say "constituents," ' " Robertson said in an interview recently. "We discussed the issues and strategy — this stuff was just part of our lives back then."

Sure, Pat played a little politics while he was growing up. Even working as a summer aide in Washington.

In 1952 he went with his father to the Democratic National Convention and the next year worked for a short time on the staff of the Senate Appropriations Committee. He also served as chairman of the Stevenson-for-President campaign on Staten Island in 1956.

It was not until he stepped into the homes of millions of Americans through his own television network that people began to notice his potential. As Michael J. Connor, staff reporter for the *Wall Street Journal,* observed on January 14, 1976, "Mr. Robertson, who ... possesses good conversational knowledge of contemporary trends, could pass for a confident and sophisticated politician."

In the spring of 1978, Robertson threw a hat into the political arena — but it was not his own. Instead, he organized a campaign for an old friend, a rather wealthy Norfolk car dealer named G. Conoly Phillips.

As one reporter stated, "Robertson selected Phillips and promoted his candidacy. The target: the Democratic nomination for his father's old seat in the Senate. In a sense it was a new round in the intra-party struggle his father had lost."

Said Megan Rosenfeld, a *Washington Post* writer, "Robertson was the brains behind the Phillips campaign. The fact that he made his (Phillips') nominating speech is evidence of his important role."

Phillips ran on an evangelical, conservative platform (rather unusual for a Virginia Democrat) and lost at the state party convention. But those who observed the campaign were duly impressed with Robertson's personal commitment and organizational ability.

The following year, in 1979, Pat was asked by *Sojourners* magazine, "Would you be surprised if you found yourself in Washington in the next decade or so?"

Answered Robertson, "If the economic and military scenario that I foresee takes place, I wouldn't be surprised if there were quite a few of us in Washington, frankly."

In 1980 the topic surfaced again. This time it was Dick Dabney, writing in the August issue of *Harper's.* "And one begins to hear talk in evangelical circles — although never from Robertson himself — that he is using the resources of CBN to run for president of the United States," he wrote.

Pat's membership in The Roundtable's Council of 56 and his subsequent resignation left many wondering if personal politics would be a part of his future.

Attorney Carl Horn, a conservative political activist from Charlotte, North Carolina, said, "I first met Pat in 1981." Horn was a guest on *The 700 Club*. He said, "We discussed, in trenchant detail, how 'the separation of church and state' had been distorted to allow ACLU lawyers to undermine our Judeo-Christian heritage."

Then, said Horn, "Several months later, I joined Pat and other Christian leaders (including Campus Crusade for Christ founder Bill Bright and the leaders of the Christian Legal Society) for a weekend retreat during which we discussed steps Christians could take to reverse this dangerous trend."

There were many at the meeting who believed that Robertson should not take a passive role on the national scene. Said Horn, "I wrote Pat after our weekend retreat and suggested that he think and pray about running for president."

About this same time, in 1981, Robertson founded an organization that would have a large influence on his own political future — the Freedom Council.

Said Oklahoma lawyer Marc Nuttle, "What the Freedom Council offers Christians is really a sixth-grade-level civics course, telling them how they can get involved in the political process."

The organization spread like a prairie fire across the nation. Soon there were chapters of the political action group in every major center of the country.

During the growth of the Freedom Council, there were those who wanted more than involvement with issues on the local front. They wanted to influence presidential politics — and Robertson, they believed, had all the right qualities. They believed he had exactly what it might take to make such a move. But as a Democrat?

Robertson soon solved that problem by adopting the

party that more closely reflected his personal views. Said his wife, Dede, "Pat might have changed my religion but I changed his politics. I was the Republican first."

It was the Freedom Council that began the early organization in Michigan. Actually, it was only one of many states where the membership, primarily interested in issues, backed specific candidates who shared their view.

In June 1985, a separate organization was formed by pro-Robertson supporters called the Committee for Freedom. It was registered with the Federal Elections Commission as a multi-candidate political action committee (PAC). Its purpose was to dispense money to conservative candidates nationwide.

Operating under the ruling that it can accept contributions of up to $5,000, as of June 1986 it had raised $353,343. Because of Robertson's surprise showing in Michigan, the media, as expected, quickly found its shovel and began to dig.

An immediate target was the Freedom Council itself. They called it a "front group" for Robertson's political aspirations. Citing that CBN had given $3 million to the Council, the *Norfolk Virginian-Pilot* said, "CBN's support for the Freedom Council is controversial because both groups are tax-exempt charitable organizations and federal law prohibits them from supporting political ambitions. Yet Freedom Council is widely credited with having mobilized thousands of precinct delegate candidates on Robertson's behalf in Michigan's early-bird August (1986) primary."

Robertson spokesman, Dave West, said, "The fact that he is president of a non-profit organization (CBN) that has definite restrictions on the kind of political activity it can engage in compounds, by two or three times, what other candidates have to deal with." West added, "Congressmen have run for high office before. The way is well charted for them."

A second controversy centered around the question of Pat's Korean military duty with the Marines in 1951. Robertson, who does not claim battle experience, says his duties included transporting classified codes between Korea and Japan.

In 1986, former Republican Congressman Paul McCloskey Jr. wrote a letter to Democratic Congressman Andrew Jacobs Jr. of Indiana, saying that Robertson (whom he sailed with to Korea on the *U.S.S. Breckinridge* with 2,000 Marines) used his father's influence to get Pat out of actual combat duty.

Robertson immediately sued McCloskey and Jacobs for $35 million each.

Said Pat, "He (Senator Robertson) was a person of the old-school South and this would have gone directly against his personal integrity. He was a very strong and powerful man and I wouldn't have dreamed of asking him that."

Explaining the suit, he told a reporter for *Time,* that McCloskey's allegations are "totally untrue."

He called them "a smear on the honor of our Marine Corps," and "... an attack by liberals to discredit me because of my strong support of national defense and our armed forces."

But, said one observer, "Pat's suit sent a strong signal to those who feel inclined to attack him. They'll think twice about it now. Lawyers are expensive."

His finances have been questioned, too. But that's nothing new. Critics have been questioning him for years. Robertson recently told *Christianity Today,* "Our 990-T Internal Revenue Service tax return is on file in every public library. An independent auditor issues quarterly statements and yearly or semi-annual audits on our operations. We're also under the scrutiny of the Federal Communications Commission."

He added, "As far as my personal finances are concerned, I would not mind releasing my income tax statements."

Even his number-one critics, People for the American Way, limit their attacks to issues. Said PAW President Anthony Podesta, "I don't know of anything in Robertson's past or present that would even create the appearance of impropriety."

By and large, Robertson discounts his detractors and has concentrated on the campaign.

It is impossible, however, for any American to run for the presidency without a strong political base. For Robertson, it was the base he had been working with for over a quarter-century.

"I'm amazed at the unanimity," says Pat. "I am being encouraged from every sector, from very conservative fundamentalists to centrist evangelicals to charismatic Pentecostals. I'm being encouraged both in white and black church groups. It seems there is a hunger in the hearts of millions of religious people for a voice to represent conservative, traditional, moral family values in our country."

Without question, the base is religious. But as Robertson's views reach new audiences through the media, his base is being widened to include those who may disagree with his theology but say "right on" to his platform.

He told *Southern Partisan,* "In speaking of issues, on *The 700 Club,* I probably deal with more different social, legislative and geo-political issues in a year than the average person would in a lifetime."

Says Robertson, "We take up every conceivable issue, analyze it, develop opinions and talk to guests. So it is a continuous education in the issues of our day. I've had various cabinet members, congressmen, foreign legislators, experts, sociologists, psychiatrists, escapees from the Soviet Union and ex-KGB men on *The 700 Club.*"

He also believes he's qualified to speak to moral issues. "I would have perhaps more of an opportunity than any other political person on the scene today to address the *morality* of budget deficits, to address the *morality* of the welfare program, to address the *morality* of our relationship with the Soviets, the *morality* of slave labor camps, the *morality* of human rights violations."

When asked about international experience, Pat points out that he:

• Has met with heads of states of many nations.
• Is an expert in the Middle East.

- Has met personally with the past three prime ministers of Israel.
- Has a corporation in South America.
- Has done business in Japan, mainland China, Hong Kong, the Philippines and more.

On the domestic front, Robertson told the *Conservative Digest* that when he lived for a time in the slums of Brooklyn, "I gained a tremendous compassion for and an understanding of the poor. The people of the neighborhood came to the parsonage to eat, to talk, to pray and to hear the Word of God. I am sincere when I say that I am no dilettante when it comes to the problems of the inner city, the difficulties of the life those people live, the many burdens and the unfairness they suffer."

He added, "When I talk about those things, I am not talking about what some liberal saw from the window of a limousine. I lived in the inner city with my family, helping my neighbors with their spiritual and other problems. Frankly, it was an invaluable experience that has served me well in the years since."

Robertson doesn't have a reputation as a braggart but on the political trail he has to make his points when he can.

Asked about his educational qualifications, he told a reporter, "Well, I would probably be the best educated president since Woodrow Wilson. I do have 10 years of higher education. I have graduate degrees in law and theology. I studied at the University of London and have four years of undergraduate work in liberal arts with a major in history."

When a Christian magazine asked him whether he had the experience to become president, Robertson said, "Frankly, I don't believe there's any job anywhere that is comparable to the presidency. So it's very difficult to say that anybody has had experience in it." He added, "I think leadership qualifications are the most important thing."

Those who have observed Robertson are impressed with his great understanding of issues and events. "When he confronts political dilemmas that our culture faces, he doesn't approach them with a broad-stroke, shallow, naive perspective," says Charles W. Jarvis, vice president of the Legal Services Corporation in Washington, D.C. "He comes with a sophisticated understanding of domestic and international economics."

As every observer of presidential politics has written, a powerful media presence is a prerequisite for success.

Robertson, without question, has gained tremendous confidence as a communicator. He has the ability not only to formulate goals — he can articulate them. That is necessary in order to gain the support of large numbers of voters.

Said Bert Lance, former director of the budget, "I give Pat Robertson high marks in a lot of different areas. One reason that political parties aren't as functional now as they used to be is that they have lost a very basic element ... the control of the flow of information to the party members. Now the one group in the country that controls the flow of information is the television evangelicals."

Fred Barnes in *The New Republic,* said, "Robertson has great political skills. He is extraordinarily genial, a trait that comes across on television. President Reagan seems dour by comparison."

But perhaps the best compliment was paid by his television sidekick, Ben Kinchlow, who recently said, "The man is honest. He will stop himself in the middle of a phrase to correct one mistake."

Looking at a possible Robertson presidency, he is constantly asked, "Would you surround yourself with only Christians?"

Pat gives this response, "I think what is needed is a unity of purpose. You have to balance the administration. You need to have a coherent policy based on shared goals and objectives."

By that, Robertson does not mean that Christianity should be imposed on people, "But it does mean that those people who are in the administration of any president should share the president's world view. If they don't they will wind up undercutting him."

Getting more specific, he recently said, "I've already made a list of my potential cabinet. One that I think very highly of is H. Ross Perot. I would like to see him as secretary of defense. I've not inquired about his religious belief but I do know that he is a wonderful patriot. And he is a conservative. I think that each president should have a cabinet that reflects his philosophical point of view."

To a reporter who asked if Pat were involved in politics to further his ministry, he said, "No. It's a new arena with different responsibilities. We already have senators and representatives who are also members of the clergy and as long as we recognize the difference in responsibilities, there should be no problem."

As attorney Carl Horn said it, "A TV preacher running for political office scares people — until they meet Pat Robertson."

On a live television program in March 1987 Robertson was asked, "Given America's historic nervousness about separation of church and state, is there any danger in a preacher being president?"

Pat replied that he's a Southern Baptist minister and that Southern Baptists — including some of his ancestors — have fought for religious freedom ever since 1780.

"We went into politics in Virginia to get the separation of church and state established. I'd fight to the death for the freedom of every single individual to worship God as he or she sees fit. I can't see any other way of living in a free country."

Jeffrey Hadden, the University of Virginia professor who has written often about Robertson, says, "Pat really sees God moving in history with a plan and America as His chosen land for its fulfillment."

On September 17, 1986, the 199th anniversary of the U.S. Constitution, Robertson gave a major address at Constitution Hall in Washington, D.C.

Over 3,000 were present. It was beamed by satellite to an additional 216 locations to an audience of over 150,000. At that event, Robertson said that he would become a declared candidate if 3 million registered voters sign petitions pledging "our prayers, our work, our gifts" to his campaign by September 17, 1987.

Standing with him on the platform was a host of conservative and evangelical leaders. Here's what Robertson told the enthusiastic audience. "We have permitted during the past 25 years an assault on our faith and values that would have been unthinkable to past generations of Americans.

"Now, in 1986 the same liberal elites that gave us the problem deny the cause and tell us that this is a problem for government.

"What we are facing is not a governmental problem, it is a moral problem. The answer lies in a new rise of faith and freedom that will give to every American a vision of hope — a vision of opportunity." The crowd roared its approval.

Former president of the Southern Baptist Convention, Jimmy Draper, who spoke at the event, said, "Pat Robertson understands the past and thus he is able to lead us into the future. He is uniquely qualified to protect us from the threats we face today."

Immediately following the Washington rally, it was announced that many of the groups seeking to support Pat's possible candidacy (including the National Committee to Draft Pat Robertson for President) were being disbanded. For the future, there would be only one group to carry out the task ahead — "Americans For Robertson."

Actually, the AFR filed a statement of organization with the Federal Elections Commission in July 1986. It was formed as an "exploratory committee" to raise and spend money on Robertson's behalf to determine if there is broad support for his candidacy. It is allowed to receive individual contributions of up to $1,000. All of its expenditures, however, count against the presidential primary spending limits from the moment of Robertson's declared candidacy.

But what about *The 700 Club?* How would he have time to host the program? At the moment he is a declared candidate, wouldn't he be forced to give equal time to others?

On September 20, 1986, at a news conference before a speech at the Economic Club of Detroit, he settled the question. "I have withdrawn as host of *The 700 Club* effective today," he announced.

Would his decision negatively affect the work of CBN? "According to a poll commissioned by CBN, 69 percent of Americans had heard of *The 700 Club*," said Robertson several months earlier, "but only 33 percent have heard of me. The thrust has been the ministry, as opposed to Pat Robertson. If I were off the scene, I don't think it would be the blow that some people think."

Said Pat in a March 1987 press interview, "I've been a broadcaster for 25 years. It's a great sacrifice to give up that kind of life for the rough and tumble of politics. But if I can do something for my children and my grandchildren to make this a better place to live, I'll do what I'm out here doing."

What does Dede think of the campaign? "I feel our nation needs the kind of leadership my husband has to offer. I think his greatest strength is in his knowledge of people and how they work and how they react. And his compassion for people."

Does Robertson believe he has got what it takes to win or at least to make an impressive showing? "You need an organization, you need a certain amount of finance and, of course, you need some media credibility to be a viable candidate," he says. "I would anticipate that would be my strong suit. It is commitment in the grass roots — and I don't think anybody else has it the way we do."

Following early caucus states of Michigan and Iowa and the primary in New Hampshire, more than one-fourth of all delegates to the nominating conventions will be selected on "Super Tuesday," March 9, 1988. The focus is on the South, with primaries that day in Alabama, Arkansas, Georgia, Florida, Kentucky, Louisiana, Mississippi, North Carolina, Tennessee and Texas. But other states add to the totals, including Maryland, Massachusetts, Missouri, Oklahoma and Rhode Island.

A Southern poll released by the *Atlanta Constitu-*

tion in March 1987 was encouraging to Robertson because 49 percent of the people in the South say they want someone who is born-again as president. About 78 percent want prayer in the schools. It also showed that the region is concerned about education, the family and crime — "About all the things that are my essential issues," says Robertson.

Nearly everyone agrees that Robertson will be the strongest in the caucus states.

Speaking about the surprise success of Pat Robertson's forces in Michigan caucuses, Senator Bob Packwood (R-Ore.) has been warning Republican regulars that the "fundamentalist network" is one that "normal politicians are unfamiliar with and it is most effective in caucus states."

When cornered about a low showing in a poll, Pat says, "The important thing is not polls, the important thing is organizing and we've out-organized everyone."

Is there another driving force behind the Robertson candidacy? Observer Garrett Epps thinks so: "Pat Robertson renounced the secular political world his father lived in, turning to the religious devotion his mother taught him. Now that he has embraced that world again, is it too speculative to think that, somewhere inside, he may want to win one for the father that he did not help in 1966?"

"Pat Robertson is the man for the hour," says former southern states Freedom Council director Dr. Bill McCormick, a former Washington lobbyist. "Leadership is built into Pat Robertson. The blood of presidents and prime ministers runs in his veins. He is the most electrifying and intellectually stimulating leader on the American scene. He epitomizes leadership in the mode of his fellow Virginian, George Washington. America is ready for fresh leadership akin to that which brought our nation into being. America needs Pat Robertson."

What are his prospects? He's established his credentials in Michigan and South Carolina.

In February 1988, another caucus state, Iowa, shows great promise. Says Robert S. Boyd of the Knight-Ridder Washington Bureau, "In Iowa, evangelical Christians and right-to-life forces give Robertson a powerful base."

And, promises Kerry Moody, Robertson field director, "We will out-organize every other candidate in Iowa. We have chairmen in two-thirds of the counties already."

Eight days later, the nation looks to the New Hampshire primary.

Boyd says, "Strong conservatives traditionally do well in New Hampshire Republican primaries and the crowd at Robertson's headquarters opening (February 11, 1987) included men and women, attracted by Robertson's views on moral issues like drugs, teenage sex and abortion."

At that event in Manchester, Robertson said, "I believe we have a date with destiny. Nothing is impossible with the spirit I feel here. We're going to win New Hampshire in 1988 and we're going to win the nomination."

2

Fireworks

In front of me, powerful spotlights at the Georgian-style Christian Broadcasting Network Center went suddenly dark.

The crowd whispered in anticipation.

Overhead — *whoosh!* — telltale, twinkling contrails gave away skyrockets shooting heavenward, then exploding into spectacular, kaleidoscopic fireworks seen at bicentennials and Fourth-of-July finales.

The vast crowd gasped in awe, an orchestra broke into a soul-stirring fanfare, and a 90-minute, nationally televised event drew to its climax.

Why on October 1, 1986, was I — a former insider of Pat Robertson's TV network — standing with thousands in the balmly Virginia Beach night air?

As the overhead explosions crescendoed, I had no trouble remembering why I was there. Exactly a quarter-century before, at 3 p.m., a few miles west of this spot, history had been made.

It was October 1, 1961. In a run-down television studio at 1318 Spratley Street in Portsmouth, Virginia, I was exhausted. We had spent all night trying to get equipment ready for a 1 p.m. debut.

Then in the final moments before our live entry to Christian broadcasting, our film projector jammed. Our hand-me-down RCA camera — our only camera — began acting up.

A local church singing group sweltered under hot

lights while we offered excuses for the increasingly frantic situation.

Finally, two hours late, Harvey Waff, our part-time engineer, threw the On-The-Air switch. But since our headsets didn't work, he only got my attention by knocking on the glass of his tiny booth. I focused the camera on a 31-year-old man standing on a makeshift set.

He had never appeared on television before, but when I gave him the hand signal, he began to smile. It wasn't an ordinary smile.

It came from deep inside — the satisfied look of a man who had faced an impossible challenge — and won.

"My name is Pat Robertson. Welcome to the Christian Broadcasting Network."

Network?

We were barely a TV station, much less a network. Yet as our creaking equipment put Pat's faint image out onto the airwaves, America's first religious television station became a reality.

Yes ... I remembered.

Now on the Virginia Beach lawn, as Pat's special guest — renowned fireworks virtuoso "Boom Boom" Zambelli — lit up the sky with a multi-rocket grand finale, my eyes were misty, my mind a whir of memories.

The smoke from the fireworks drifted away and one of the many CBN executives whose names I don't even know anymore turned to me and said, "You've got to hand it to him. It's hard to believe how far it's all come."

Indeed, I agreed with the young man. How far Pat had come ... Marion Gordon "Pat" Robertson ...

- *once an embarrassment to his prominent United States senator father;*
- *once a hard-drinking party boy;*
- *once a Yale Law School graduate who in a fit of self-sacrificing idealism had sold his possessions and moved his young family to the slums of Brooklyn to suffer with the poor;*
- *once an unknown preacher who would two*

> decades later be voted "Charismatic Leader
> of the Decade" by a neo-Pentecostalist mag-
> azine;
> • once a troubled businessman whose wife
> pondered divorce ...

Yes, Pat had built a major television network, a respected graduate university, and had gone on to be named
among "America's Ten Most Admired Men" by *Good
Housekeeping* magazine, to be called "a powerful presence on the platform and on television" by *U.S. News
and World Report* — and named one of the "25 most intriguing Americans" in the gossipy *People* magazine.

Earlier in the celebration, I had been ushered onto the
high-tech set of *The 700 Club,* CBN's flagship program.
It is carried on 199 U.S. and Canadian stations as well as
stations reaching many other nations, and is seen on the
CBN Cable Network, which includes more than 7,000
cable systems serving 78 million viewers.

There I saw my old friend with his greying hair, his
gentle, friendly grin and his retinue of co-hosts, efferves-
cent Danuta Soderman and folksy Ben Kinchlow.

Under the bright television lights, they were in the
midst of the show's magazine format, designed with a
unique mix of information and inspiration — as well as a
guest list that rivals the Today Show's or Good Morning
America's — presidents and preachers, Soviets and sociologists, authors and icthyologists, Bible smugglers and
creationist biologists ... spies and sports celebrities.

I was up next.

"It's the National Counseling Center that makes it
still worth the effort," whispered an old friend at my elbow. "Last year we had over 4 million calls" — people
who call during the show seeking help. "We've saved
marriages, helped drug addicts, and referred people to all
kinds of social agencies."

"Once," he said, "I talked to a guy in Houston who
had a gun to his head. Ready to blow his brains out. I
held him on the line while we got a local counselor to
rush to his apartment. We saved the man's life."

That day of our first broadcast, just *one* phone call had been cause for celebration. But today in the United States alone there are 25 full-time and 20 part-time phone centers taking steady calls from viewers wanting help or just an understanding ear.

I smiled wistfully as I looked around. Today's CBN facility employs hundreds of professionals. *The 700 Club* set rivals that of any network talk show — in a studio that is light-years away from that dowdy little set-up where everything started in 1961.

Out under the bright lights, Pat was in a nostalgic mood as he reviewed events that had led to today's celebration. He talked with Dick Simmons, with whom the Robertsons had shared a rat-infested apartment in New York. With Dan Morstad, an early volunteer cameraman who became inspired to begin a major crisis-intervention center in Minneapolis.

Then Danuta said, "Now we want you to meet the first full-time employee of CBN, Neil Eskelin." And I was ushered out onto the carpet and into an overstuffed chair to reminisce about the not-so-distant, not-so-glittery, good ol' days. Pat's first question was one I had been asked before, but not by him. "Neil, did you have any idea in those early days that all of this would come about?"

"Well," I answered carefully, "I certainly didn't see all of the brick and mortar as it stands today."

My mission had been a labor of love in those days. I had lived with him and his family back when he couldn't pay me enough to meet even room-and-board basics.

I smiled. "But," I quipped, "it would have been impossible to work 16 hours a day for practically no money if we did not feel something important was taking place."

Here I was again with this impressive man — this 6-foot-1 father of four, this lawyer and economist with deep-set eyes.

And I recounted how my tenure with him had begun three months before our first signal hit the airwaves, and had continued that first year of operation.

What I did not tell viewers was that from the moment

I first met him, I knew Marion Gordon Robertson was no ordinary broadcaster.

How did I know? And why had I placed such confidence in this man who had been working night and day to make a vision become reality?

How could I have foreseen all of this? Today his impact is being felt in ever-widening circles — and increasingly outside of "religious" circles.

Larry Sabato, political scientist at the University of Virginia, puts it like this: "Pat's an excellent orator, even spellbinding. On television he's smooth, sharp and genial — like Reagan."

Like Ronald Reagan ...

Pat has become a gifted multi-media communicator with a vision for America and a respect for her past, for days when forefathers declared it a Christian nation, when *"In God We Trust"* was put on money without apology, when *"under God"* was inserted into the Pledge of Allegiance.

Those who have worked closely with Pat will tell you: "He's a hard-nosed businessman and a tough negotiator."

Add to that his profound grasp of economics, his background in law, and his political savvy. The CBN Cable Network is one of America's biggest success stories in the rapidly growing cable television industry. Robertson jumped into satellite technology early, building an earth station in 1977. The coast-to-coast, 24-hour network pioneered the concept of bringing quality family programming back to American television. *"The Family Entertainer,"* as it is called, has become one of the largest satellite-to-cable services in the United States.

CBN Cable's dramatic rise is due to Pat's decision to give the public what it wanted to see. Westerns such as *The Monroes* and *Wagon Train.* A family hour with *Gentle Ben* and *Here Come the Brides.* Classic movies starring John Wayne and Maureen O'Hara. Children's programming from *Romper Room* to *Flipper.* Specials like the *Grand Champion Tennis Tour* and the *Grand Prix Horse Jumping Classics.* Classic comedies from the

George Burns and Gracie Allen Show to *Bachelor Father*. Plus game shows, news and a whole lot more.

The Nielsen Home Video Index reported that CBN Cable became the top-rated basic cable network during cable's peak viewing hours.

When Robertson opened an office on Madison Avenue to tell his story, national accounts began signing on. CBN advertising clients now read like a list of the "Fortune 500." Hershey Foods, Scott Paper, Johnson & Johnson, Chevrolet, Merrill Lynch, Mobil Oil, Seven-Up, Pilsbury, E.F. Hutton, General Mills.

For years, rating services had written off religious-oriented shows as having an audience so small it could hardly be measured. But something didn't add up. As one CBN executive put it, "How can the rating services say we have 435,000 viewers, when our donor list is actually larger?" To be precise, analysis by the American Resource Bureau on data from A.C. Nielsen company in February 1983 stated that the estimated number of households who watched *The 700 Club* in one week was 408,000.

Critics such as Jeffrey Hadden, sociologist at the University of Virginia, were blasting the so-called "electronic evangelists" for grossly overstating the actual size of their audiences. CBN's research staff, meanwhile, was raising questions of its own. David Clark, the network's vice president for marketing, who has a doctorate in communications from the University of Iowa, was asking, "Why are so many of our affiliates not included in the numbers?" And "Why don't they include our satellite network in the ratings?"

In 1985, Nielsen was commissioned to conduct a national study that, for the first time, included both cable and broadcast audiences. I attended the press conference in Georgia when the landmark study was made public.

The 40-page report was an eye-opener to say the least.

It showed 4.4 million people in the United States watch *The 700 Club* every day. Also, the research concluded that, on average, 27 million Americans watch at least a portion of the program each month (an unduplicated audience for a minimum of six minutes at one time).

The Nielsen study went on to show that at least 40 percent of the nation tunes in to the top 10 media ministries at least once a month. And that's just the top 10. When the hundreds of other broadcasters are included, it is obvious that well over half of all United States adults watch this type of programming. That's called a *majority*.

Jeff Hadden was at the press conference. But he had changed his tune. He told a reporter from *Time* magazine the 1985 Nielsen report shows a "much larger" audience than he and other experts had thought. The preachers, he said, "have greater unrestricted access to media than any other interest group in America." Powered by TV evangelism, he predicts, the Christian right "is destined to become the major social movement in America" during the late 20th century.

From the moment the report was released, the media began taking a new look at the power of these personalities — especially Robertson.

Did I know all this would happen? Out under the bright lights, as Pat's warm smile drew me out of my reverie, I didn't voice questions I and many have begun to ask. No, it was a day of celebration.

And the answers would not be easy or simple. I know personally that trying to categorize Pat is difficult. To his staff, he is an executive. To the students at his university, he is an academician. To a large television audience, he is a source of inspiration. To evangelical America, he is a leading spokesman. Cory SerVaas, M.D., publisher of *The Saturday Evening Post,* merely calls him "an unusual man — a broadcaster, a lawyer, an economist, a theologian, a businessman."

Later as I loitered around the facility, I could not help but be awed. Located just off a major expressway, the sprawling CBN Center is impressive by any standard. Cut into a pine forest on several hundred acres are handsome brick buildings that resemble nearby colonial Williamsburg.

Holly hedges, brick sidewalks, magnolias, and crepe myrtles add to the landscape.

The 700 Club originates from CBN's headquarters, an imposing structure with huge limestone columns at the entrance. Across the campus are equally striking buildings housing the university administration, classrooms and library.

"If you look at Pat's background, it's only natural for him to build a university," a college professor from North Carolina told me. "Phi Beta Kappa at Washington and Lee. Law degree from Yale. He was raised around the academic life and now he's got the reason and the resources to do it himself."

Robertson began to express his deep-seated desire to build a university back in the mid-1970s. This was not to be an ordinary college. In fact, there would be no undergraduate program at all. It would offer only master's degrees and above.

On TV, Pat began sharing his concept. "We need moral leadership in every area of public life. In the media, in business, in government, in education," he said.

Almost immediately, applications began coming from students across the country. Graduates from many of the nation's leading colleges made the decision to attend the school dubbed simply "CBN University."

In 1978, the doors opened to its first graduate school — the School of Communication — with 77 full-time students. Other major programs were soon to follow: The School of Education in 1980, Schools of Business and Biblical Studies in 1982, the School of Public Policy in 1983, and the Institute of Journalism in 1984.

In 1984, another milestone was reached. CBNU was granted full accreditation by the Southern Association of Colleges and Schools. That is the highest accreditation available to any academic institution in America.

The program, however, that gives Robertson deep personal satisfaction is the one that admitted over 100 students in September 1986, the School of Law.

At the time of the anniversary broadcast, CBNU had already graduated 580 students. As I had waited to go on camera, a production assistant had touched my elbow, "Take a look at this," she said, as she pointed to a monitor. It was a video review of the worldwide projects Robertson has launched through CBN.

One is called Operation Blessing. Started in 1978, it has helped distribute more than $140 million in food, clothing, shelter, medicines and financial aid to more than 24 million people in many parts of the world — including Ethiopian refugees, American farmers in crisis, earthquake victims in Mexico City and San Salvador ... as well as ordinary people struggling to put food on their tables or to pay heating bills.

People who need food, shelter, or medical attention.

People with deep needs. Here's one case a CBN staffer described.

"Debi was in trouble. She'd been out of a job for three months and she desperately needed help to pay the bills for her disabled husband and the three children. The government said they couldn't help and she had no family to turn to in her time of need. So Debi called on Operation Blessing for assistance. And in a very short amount of time, she had the help she needed."

Here's what Debi wrote CBN: "I'm sending a letter to let you know how much I appreciated your love and financial help. I was so happy to hear my landlord say he was touched to see ... that Operation Blessing would send a check to him on behalf of me for back rent." Her letter concluded, "I would like you to know that about two days after I asked for help, I got a good job. Now I can support my disabled husband and three children. Thanks again."

The ongoing program involves thousands of people from all walks of life who volunteer to be part of this outreach to those in need — plumbers, doctors, lawyers, housewives, mechanics, and many more. When the program began, needs were simply matched with gifts. But now, with Operation Blessing's network of volunteers, hundreds of unique problems can be given that personal touch.

On the studio monitors, the next video feature concerned a program called "Heads Up." It is Robertson's attack on illiteracy in America. Why is Pat concerned? According to CBN research, "27 million people in America are functionally illiterate — and there are an additional 46 million people who operate at a marginal level of literacy. It's estimated that illiteracy costs American taxpayers $224 billion a year in crime, welfare payments, lost revenue and remedial literacy programs."

The problem, however, is much greater than statistics indicate, "because no one can begin to put a price tag on the insecurity, the loneliness, the terror of not being able to read a bus sign or a road map or an employment application."

Here's how the Heads Up program fights the problem. It uses a phonics-based reading program called "Sing, Spell, Read & Write," developed by a teacher named Sue Dickson. The approach uses "catchy songs, games, storybooks, workbooks and prizes to teach reading skills." The program is fun — and it works.

In its first few months of operation, Heads Up has brought reading literacy to over 100,000 people.

"When Robertson zeros in on an idea," said a former employee, "you'd better not stand in his way. He's going to make it happen."

A good example is what he's done with *The Book*.

As CBN's David Clark told a reporter, "In the early 1980s ... Robertson had a vision to place the Bible and its remarkable story into the hands and minds of the everyday man and woman and child."

The result was a version that reads straight through, like a book — with no dividing lines down the page.

According to Clark, CBN has spent over $6 million in promotion. You've seen the spots on all the major networks. And already, *The Book* has sold over 2 million copies.

Clark added, "Often while doing an interview with secular reporters, Pat would realize by their answers that they had no idea what the Bible says. From this kind of response and the results of the Gallup poll, he concluded that our nation is biblically illiterate."

That's frustrating for a man who moves with ease from secular to spiritual conversation. Says one associate, "Pat can talk about photography one minute and prophecy the next. What he can't understand is why other people can't do the same." In a Christian nation, he believes, discussing religious issues should be as natural as breathing.

His focus, however, doesn't end with United States issues. Pat's vision is global. CBN is involved in 71 countries of the world. Here are just a few examples: Greenland, North America — Armed Forces Radio and Television Service; Atghanistan, Asia — short wave radio; Colombia, South America — 27 video centers; Nigeria, Africa — *World News This Week,* an African news program; Venezuela, South America — airing the animated *Superbook;* plus projects in Japan, Argentina, El Salvador, Namibia, England and 61 other nations.

Without doubt, Robertson's most sensitive foreign operation is in the Middle East. On hand for the celebration was George Otis, whose High Adventure organization literally *gave* CBN a TV station in south Lebanon in 1982. Middle East Television sends its programming into Lebanon, Israel, Syria and Jordan. But the powerful signal has also been seen in Iran, Kuwait, Saudi Arabia, Libya, Cyprus, Turkey and Egypt. Breaking the language barriers can be tough, but as a CBN programmer said, "We get their attention with *Championship Wrestling,* then give them *The 700 Club.*" The station is no stranger to fireworks either, having been the target of bombs on more than one occasion.

When the anniversary edition of *The 700 Club* had concluded, I was driven with other guests to the Robertson's home for lunch. It wasn't far. The three-story, five-bedroom residence is on the CBN grounds. Pat's wife, Dede, greeted me just inside the door.

"Neil, it's a little bigger than the house in Portsmouth," she said with a laugh. My mind flashed back to the time I lived with them in a house with cracks so wide in the floorboards the silverware could drop through to the ground.

Dede has fought some of life's toughest battles as Pat pursued his vision. Their marriage was on the verge of divorce when he went into the ministry. She once confided how she had believed Pat had lost his mind because of his newfound religious call.

"Do we have discussions?" she once repeated as she considered a reporter's query. "No, we have arguments. We used to argue about the car. He always had it. Now we argue about how much time we should spend with the family." Then she added, "I still don't win many."

Their oldest son, Tim, just a kid when I knew him, is now president of CBN. Pat is chairman of the board.

The little daughter I remembered, Elizabeth, lives in Dallas where she is operations manager for a television station. Son Gordon is a lawyer in Norfolk and lives at home. Youngest daughter, Anne, works with the seminar program for the "partners" — contributors — of CBN.

That day of the anniversary celebration was an unusually hot day, in the 90s. Lunch was served on the patio. To one side of the beautiful garden were the stables — Pat always has been keen on horses. The topic at the table was politics. Pat said, "I just can't believe the reception we're getting around the country. The crowds are so enthusiastic." He said, "I'm just amazed."

Then the topic turned to finances and accountability. "The press just won't let up," he said. "I'm not sure they'll ever be satisfied."

His present living quarters are a good example.

Built in 1983, the impressive residence has been a constant target of secular journalists attempting to tell the "real story" of the Christian operation. Once CBN had to issue an official statement about Robertson's home. It read, "The CBN University chancellor's residence is constructed in keeping with the other buildings of CBN University and the Christian Broadcasting Network.

"It will be used for student and faculty functions of the expanding university, for hosting visiting speakers and other official purposes."

To Robertson, it is in keeping with the lifestyle of any corporate leader of an operation with an income of

It was a rugged life, with the Robertsons moving from place to place. Willis often talked of sparse meals of sorghum and sweet potatoes. As a lad, he spent many mornings feeding the horses and cutting firewood.

The family moved to Lynchburg, Virginia, when Willis was only four years old and then on to a tiny congregation in Franklin County, which was so poor it didn't have a high school. Pat isn't the first one in his family known for fund-raising. His grandmother organized a play, "The Turn of the Tide," which raised enough money to build a three-room, three-teacher school.

Willis was admitted to the University of Richmond at the age of 16. He scored so well on the admissions test — based on Shakespeare's plays — that he was placed in second-year classes.

He was also quite an athlete. He was a right tackle in football and made the tennis and track teams. His days of chopping wood gave him the strength to be a hammer thrower. He holds the all-time University of Richmond record, hurling the hammer 136 feet. The record remains intact since the university dropped the event as being too dangerous.

He graduated from college and began to practice law the same year, 1908. He began politics in 1912 when he campaigned at a political rally to become a delegate for Woodrow Wilson at the Virginia state convention.

As he once recalled, "The mass meeting was controlled by Wilson's foes, but I made such a fuss that they said if I'd just quiet down they'd let me go as one delegate with three against me." By 1916 he was serving in the Virginia Senate.

Then, there was that special woman:

Gladys Churchill Willis was born in Switzerland-on-the-St. Johns, Florida. She grew up in Alabama in an academic, cultured Southern environment. An aunt founded both Judson and Howard College for Boys. Her grandfather was a professor at Judson.

Her deep religious faith was partly a product of family influence. Her father, John Milton Willis, who gradu-

over $200 million annually. But the facts are that Pat is paying for the home with book royalties and is giving it to CBN University.

In return he lives rent-free. Robertson's salary, recently listed as $60,335 for 1986, is a relatively modest sum for the head of such a major corporation. His lifestyle reflects standards he has set for the entire organization. As a corporate executive, he has access to a 22-year-old, 24-seat BAC-111 jet formerly owned by Metro-Goldwyn-Meyer and country superstar Kenny Rogers.

The fact is that anyone who has as much TV exposure as Robertson has celebrity status in this country. As a result, the potential for personal income is almost limitless.

An aide told me, "He turns down hundreds of speaking engagements every year. If he were looking for income, there are dozens of things he would be doing."

As I looked the house over, I could not help but realize that the real question is one of motive:

• Did Pat make a decision to build a television network for personal gain? To his supporters, the answers are obvious. But the news media isn't as kind.

• How important are his material possessions? The media would paint him as a rich scion of Virginia society who has gone on to make it big in the religion business.

But I had other questions:

√ Had Pat changed? I remembered a selfless, driven man.

√ Had big budgets and power blurred his vision? The man I remembered was not one whose head could be turned by fame and money. And now, there's this talk of the White House.

√ Was the simple preacher-with-a-dream now a big-time power broker? No, I said to myself. Not Pat. Not the old Pat I knew and respected.

And what about:

• *His father who suffered a bitter political setback? What caused that? Is Pat trying to avenge his father's defeat?*

• *His wedding that neither his nor Dede's parents*

attended. After all, Dede comes from the cream of Ohio affluent society and Pat is the descendant of a Virginia political dynasty.

• Pat's failed bar exam. What happened? What does it say about the man?

• His abrupt change in lifestyle and career following a meeting in a Philadelphia restaurant. What happened there? What made Pat change course?

I left the anniversary celebrations with many questions ...

Does America really know this man?

I felt compelled to examine the beliefs of this oft-criticized American defended so compellingly by his vast audience of television viewers — and criticized so roundly by a national media that seemingly hasn't approved of a national leader since the assassination of John F. Kennedy.

What generates the cheers and controversy?

I resolved to look at what really happened in Michigan on May 27, 1986. Is Pat Robertson destined for the White House? Is he deserving of such an office? If he doesn't win the nomination on his first try, will he attempt again?

But basically, I asked myself as I gazed out at the twinkling lights of the CBN complex:

Just who is Pat Robertson today?

3

Royal Blood

Springtime had already come to Virginia's be Shenandoah Valley when Marion Gordon Roberts born in Lexington on March 22, 1930.

His parents, A. Willis and Gladys Robertso from a long line of notable Americans.

Pat's mother had a special fascination with gy. The family tree includes such names as U. dents William Henry Harrison (ninth presider and Benjamin Harrison (23rd president, 1889-18 former is best remembered as "Tippecanoe," a given after defeating the Shawnee Indians in 18 battle of Tippecanoe.

His grandson, Benjamin, won the preside the help of a Republican campaign son "Grandfather's Hat Fits Ben."

Roots of the tree include another Benjamir (William Henry's father) who served in the C Congresses and signed the Declaration of Inde And it goes back to names such as William Ch John Armistead, members of the governin Burgesses before 1700.

Pat's father was elected to the U.S. Hous sentatives when Pat was only two years old. F fore that, Willis was making quite a name for was born the son of a Baptist minister in N West Virginia, on May 27, 1887. His fath Pierce Robertson, was a "home missionary poverished mountain villages of that area.

ated from the University of Richmond, was a trial lawyer. But in his middle years he turned his back on law to become a minister.

"When you look at Pat's family background," noted one observer, "you find so many parallels. It seems history really does repeat itself — especially in Pat's case."

Gladys attended Hollins College in Roanoke, but it was much earlier that she met Willis Robertson. They were fourth cousins.

"We were almost reared together," she recalled. "He used to help me with my Latin."

She told a time when they were courting and he told her he was going to quit politics for good. That was back in 1919.

She used to laugh about it. "He couldn't possibly have left politics."

Their wedding took place in Petersburg, when he was in the Virginia Senate. They moved to Lexington and there they had two sons, A. Willis Jr. — today an investment banker in Atlanta — and Marion Gordon.

They remained in Lexington even after 1926 when Willis accepted a post as chairman of the Virginia State Commission of Game and Inland Fisheries, which required him to spend time in Richmond.

It was a job that he enjoyed, for Willis Robertson loved the outdoors — and particularly hunting. One dismal day in February, he and a colleague were stalking birds in South Carolina.

"It started raining," the friend recalled, "but we kept going through the woods. We got wetter and wetter. It was really pretty miserable.

"We got involved in some moss bogs, which didn't help any. The deeper we got into the woods, the darker it got. I could see the flash of Willis' gun.

"Finally, I said to him that I appreciated his bringing me along on this hunting trip, but it was so ugly that I thought I'd turn back.

"Willis looked at me and said, 'Well, all right, if you want to throw away the rest of the afternoon.' "

His love for the outdoors followed his entire life,

from the time when quail hung in bunches in butcher shops and sold two for a quarter. Recalling those days, he once said, "I knew we weren't going to have any game unless we had some laws."

One of his first acts when he went to the Virginia State Senate in 1916 had been to propose a bill creating the State Fish and Game Department. When he later became its commissioner, he spent several enjoyable years working on programs to populate rivers with trout and woods with wild turkeys and quail.

The story is told of him in 1945 speaking before the Army Corps of Engineers in opposition to a dam that was planned across the beautiful Shenandoah River in Virginia's Clarke County. A news photographer was there to record Robertson's fighting stance, his right fist clenched and extended.

At that hearing, Willis said, "The last command of the immortal Stonewall Jackson, uttered in his delirium in the farmhouse at Guinea Station, was, 'General Pender, you must hold your ground,' and that, gentlemen, is what we intend to do."

As a freshman U.S. congressman in 1932, he organized the Wildlife Committee and, as its first chairman, cosponsored the Pittman-Robertson Act taxing sporting goods for conservation. He also wrote and helped to pass the Duck Stamp Bill for game refuges.

The person who had named him in 1926 to the Virginia State Commission of Game and Inland Fisheries was Harry S. Byrd — a longtime friend.

Byrd and Robertson were born two weeks apart in Martinsburg. They lived on the same street and were delivered by the same physician. They were seatmates in the Virginia Senate for six years. And they were elected to Congress in the same year, 1932.

Byrd went to the Senate, Robertson to the House.

There the friendship ended.

The boyhood pals became bitter rivals.

Both were Democrats — but were poles apart on the issues. Byrd turned to the left, while Robertson voted against the "New Deal."

In 1946, there was a special election held to fill the unexpired U.S. Senate seat of Carter Glass. The candidate — hand-chosen by Byrd — hit a wall of opposition at the state convention.

Robertson was the second choice.

He won the nomination and entered the Senate — without Byrd's blessing.

Gladys did not care for life in Washington, so she and the youngsters returned to Lexington. The freshman senator took up residence in a basement room in a hotel near Capitol Hill and returned home on weekends.

Writer Margaret Wilkins visited Pat's mother and wrote: "... for 36 years the senator from Virginia has been a familiar figure around Washington, but his wife has not been there for the past 15 years or more.

"Instead, she has chosen the seclusion of the couple's 10-room home in Lexington, where she lives quietly and, for the most part, alone. Neighbors say they rarely see her."

Wilkins described her as "wearing a blue sweater and skirt and bright lipstick that complimented her white hair."

She gave her impression of the house:

"Flanking the fireplace were two handsome original paintings of the school of Tintoretto, in standing frames. A portrait of the senator gazed down from the adjacent wall."

The rest of the room "was filled with signed photographs of some of the personalities the Robertsons have known: Queen Mother Elizabeth, John F. Kennedy, Winston Churchill and others. Sir Winston was a cousin, a fact carefully noted in the family genealogy."

Those who remember her talk about her soft speech that had traces of her Alabama upbringing.

And they talk about her "precise language" that was credited to her literary father. They said she expressed herself in a wide vocabulary that was completely natural to her.

But it is her spiritual side that people talk about most — especially since it had such an influence on Pat.

She never thought it foolish that her youngest son would spend years of his life in a project most people did not understand.

In her later years, she once said, "I'm a complete idiot about my boys and I don't care who knows it. They are the kind of sons any woman would be proud of. And I have a special interest in Pat's work ... such a great cause."

Talking about her faith, a family friend said, "She was about the most religious person I knew. She was a Baptist, but not your average Baptist. She didn't just talk the talk, she walked the walk."

Gladys was known to spend a rather large part of her time praying and reading the Bible. "When you talked with her, you had the feeling that she had some special connection with God," recalled one acquaintance. "But I'll say this, people didn't laugh about her faith. They knew it was real. She was greatly respected by everybody in town."

She once said, "Some years ago, when I stopped being just a church member and started being a Christian, I realized that one cannot be spiritual and worldly at the same time."

Gladys was quick, however, to defend herself from occasional implications that she was too remote from the political scene.

She told the reporter, "In these days, communication is so rapid that distance does not cut one off from information. I know what is going on in Washington and what is before Congress. I read every newspaper and magazine I can, and I seldom miss the radio and television newscasts."

She continued, "I chose this life myself. I believe I am more effective right here in Lexington, where I am closer to the constituents. I am able to route many of the inquiries to my husband or to the proper departments of government."

Indeed, she was one of her husband's staunchest supporters.

Garett Epps, author of *The Shad Treatment,* a novel

of Virginia politics, once wrote in the *Washington Post,* "In the Senate, A. Willis Robertson fit smoothly into the powerful 'Southern caucus,' and by the late '50s he became chairman of the powerful Banking and Commerce Committee.

"Tightly conservative on fiscal issues, he also supported a strong military defense."

What the elder Robertson stood for is evident in the address he gave April 27, 1947, at Cape Henry, Virginia, a historic spot not far from the present CBN Center. It was on that day, 340 years earlier, that the first Virginia settlers had landed.

He said, "The philosophy of ancient Greece was 'know thyself,' of ancient Rome, 'discipline thyself.' But the philosophy of the Christian religion, upon which a new experiment in self-government was to be founded, was symbolized by the cross erected on this spot by the first settlers — 'give thyself.' "

He also enjoyed quoting patriot Patrick Henry when he said, "I speak now, no longer as a Virginian. I now and henceforth shall speak as an American."

He once said, "In two global wars we have fought to preserve the principles of our founding fathers and yet the world peace for which we sacrificed blood and treasure eludes our grasp."

He added, "Instead of the world being made safe for democracy we find today the totalitarian and anti-God ideology of communism feeding on the measureless misery of war-torn countries in Europe, while many of our own people have so lost faith in the fact that God governs in the affairs of men they think another armed conflict is inevitable.

"After the atomic bomb tests at Bikini, Admiral Blandy said: 'Civilization faces the choice of living under God or of living underground.' "

His label was that of a Democrat, but at times you would never know it. In fact, Robertson was an early supporter of General Dwight D. Eisenhower as a Democratic candidate for president.

In 1948, Robertson told Douglas Southall Freeman,

a Virginia newspaper editor, that the general was the only man who could unite the nation and deal with the Soviet Union. He urged his Southern colleagues to draft Eisenhower at the Democratic National Convention, but they didn't follow his advice.

When Ike declared he was a Republican, Robertson confidentially contacted financier Bernard Baruch in October 1951 and asked him to promote Eisenhower as the 1952 Republican candidate.

The rift between Robertson and Byrd continued to widen. As Epps points out:

"• Byrd opposed the Marshall Plan, Robertson supported it;

"• Byrd talked openly of purging the junior senator in 1954 from the ranks of the Democratic party. But Robertson resisted, and by primary time, one wag said, 'He had hunted or prayed with everyone in the state.' The purge effort was quietly dropped."

• A. Willis was against big government. Byrd was for it.

• In 1957 Robertson successfully opposed federal construction of a hydroelectric dam at Hell's Canyon, Idaho. He maintained that the project could be more justifiably left to private enterprise. Byrd supported the project.

Robertson became chairman of the Banking and Currency Committee in 1958.

It was from that position that he became the leading spokesman for the conservative coalition of Southern Democrats and Republicans on fiscal matters.

Then, the government deficit was only $12.9 billion. But Robertson warned, "If that deficit continues to rise, foreign and domestic capital will flee from the dollar."

Unlike Byrd, he only gave nominal endorsement to Senator John F. Kennedy's presidential candidacy in 1960. He did it as a gesture of party loyalty.

He persistently opposed Kennedy administration programs in Congress.

According to *Congressional Quarterly,* Robertson was among the three Senate Democrats who most often voted against Kennedy-supported bills in 1962 and 1963. Byrd announced his retirement from the Senate in 1965, and, as was possible with his enormous political power, he arranged that his son, Harry Byrd Jr., be appointed to take his place.

So, in 1966, the stage was set for the final attack.

The Byrd organization began openly talking of dumping the 79-year-old Robertson for a younger man in the primaries.

Willis refused to bow out.

The Byrd organization withheld its support and helped propel the challenger, William B. Spong Jr., into the race.

It was a bitter primary campaign fought as viciously as any in Virginia political history. To make it worse, Robertson's main opposition was from Portsmouth, the very community where Pat was building his television network. But in this race, Pat stayed on the sidelines, feeling that his number-one priority was CBN.

Pat said, "I did write one speech for him ... but most of my efforts on his behalf were very frustrating."

Willis turned for support to the same constituency that had been his base for over 40 years, the conservationists.

In fact, he had been named the nation's leading conservationist by *Field and Stream* magazine. Those huntsmen and fishermen had been by his side in the past, and he certainly needed them now. Plus, he had the experience.

"Robertson had that powerful position as Chairman of the Senate Banking and Currency Commission to oversee expenditures on housing, unemployment, and to recommend controls on exports, prices, wages, and borrowing," Epps says. "He had built a respected reputation as an expert on foreign trade, tariffs, banking, currency and taxation. These were subjects that many senators often seemed reluctant to pursue."

There are many who remember his campaign style. As observer Ben Beagle tells it, "He did not wear linen suits, nor a floppy hat. And nobody ever compared him to 'Big Daddy' down on the old plantation. The white hair and blue eyes were combined with a conservative suit. Robertson looked like a U.S. senator, a business executive, and the lawyer he was." But he would still call on Stonewall Jackson to make his points.

As expected, Robertson's age became one of the campaign issues. But a few days before the election, his opponent stopped talking about it. The age factor was made clear when the elder Byrd, two weeks younger than Robertson, slipped into a coma.

As Pat recalled in his book *Shout It From the Housetops,* "The primary was held in July on the hottest day of the year. I drove up to his campaign headquarters in Richmond to be with him when the returns came in. But as the day wore on, something was obvious. Because of the heat, a lot of older people who would have voted for him simply did not turn out at the polls.

"The people along the coast sensed a kill and turned out in droves, while his supporters in the mountain regions and the seventh district, thinking he was strong enough to win without them, stayed away from the polls."

When the votes had been counted, out of 433,159 ballots cast, Robertson lost by 611. As Pat recalled later, "It really crushed him. He had given his whole life to public service."

More important, as Pat remembers:

"Something very important left him."

Willis Robertson went into unwilling retirement.

For a while, he served as a consultant for the International Bank of Reconstruction and Development in Washington.

But he spent a lot of time hunting pheasants.

Then, Gladys Robertson passed away in Lexington on April 18, 1968.

The day of the funeral was meaningful for Pat. For the first time, Willis Robertson asked his son to pray with him that he might know the God his wife knew.

To Pat Robertson, that was more important than a television network or a political campaign. It meant that the two people who had given him life would spend eternity together.

Willis died of a heart condition on November 1, 1971 at the age of 84. He was buried at the Stonewall Jackson Memorial Cemetery in Lexington.

Today his portrait hangs in Richmond at the Virginia State Game and Island Fisheries Commission.

Says Pat, "What influenced me was his tremendous integrity and his sense of the history of this country." In addition, "He did not like government intervention in the affairs of people and I think he's passed that on to me."

Historian J. Harvie Wilkinson said he "personified Spartan discipline, pioneer individualism and Calvinistic morality."

The day after his passing, the *New York Times* wrote, "Many of Mr. Robertson's predictions over the state of the American economy in the early 1960s have been fulfilled in recent years, especially the instability of the dollar on the world market, continuing inflation fueled by rising federal deficit, and increased spending."

Senator John Stennis, from Mississippi, recalls, "He had a quote from the Bible for many things. But Robertson's true passion was interpreting the Constitution. He almost worshipped the Constitution and had a fine knowledge of it, too."

Stennis added, "I have never had a finer friend or finer associate. I loved him dearly."

Even the man who so narrowly defeated him, William Spong, said, "I found him to be a man of deep spiritual conviction ... and a clean political opponent."

As a longtime resident of Lexington told me, "Pat's father was a remarkable individual. And it is so interesting to see how Pat has become more and more like him as the years go by. I guess that when law and economics and government are such a part of your family discussion, it really rubs off."

Then he added, "Pat may be known as a television minister, but I don't see him as that at all. He's more like his father ...

"With his mother's religious side thrown in."

4

Party Boy

"When I was in college I used to come home staggering drunk at three or four o'clock in the morning and my mother would be up," Pat once told a CBN audience.

"But she never stopped praying. When I went to law school, and on, she always prayed. I didn't read all those little books she sent me. I was really embarrassed about all that foolishness. But I couldn't get away from her prayers."

Pat was her youngest. Her little boy.

As a youngster, having a father in Congress didn't seem to go to his head. "He was just one of the boys," remembers chum Buddy Glasgow.

"He wasn't that fast on his feet," also recalls Glasgow, now an insurance executive in Griffin, Georgia. "In fact, he was a little heavy. So we'd use him as a guard or a tackle. Our houses weren't too far apart. So when we were growing up, we spent a lot of time playing football or baseball in the yard. That was before TV, so we spent a lot of time together. He was a great sport."

Since Pat skipped a grade in school, most of his childhood pals were older than he was, but he'd stand right up to them, recalls another friend.

He organized a "Robertson for Congress" club among sixth-grade classmates. Except for the short time the family was in Washington, most of Pat's schooling was in the affluent, culture-minded town that is home to two of the South's most prestigious colleges — Washington and Lee University and Virginia Military Institute.

"The town had roots," notes one friend. "His family

had roots, too." And Pat's mother took great pride in those roots, reminding her sons of their colonial, Southern and Virginia heritages.

"Pat was quite a singer," recalls high school cohort George Lauderdale. "He was a real ham on stage." Pat played the leading role in the school's production of *H.M.S. Pinafore,* a light-hearted Gilbert and Sullivan musical.

"Pat looked so handsome in his captain's uniform," recalls schoolmate Julia Lewis Smith Martin. "We thought we were real professionals. You see, we had a marvelous music teacher and she would put on some really outstanding productions. Lexington is a very small town, but a unique town because of the two colleges" — VMI and Washington and Lee. "The learning atmosphere of the colleges spills over into the town so you have a higher cultural environment than you would have, say, in a mill town."

Martin is now with the public information office at VMI. "Lexington is only 7,500 people, but we have our own symphony orchestra. And we have at least three amateur theater groups. So you see, Pat was raised in a unique community."

Robertson did not graduate from Lexington High School.

In his junior year, he was sent off to a boarding school, McCallie Prep, in Chattanooga, Tennessee — to be groomed for college. The headmaster of the school, Dr. William Pressly, reflects the proud sense of tradition of the region.

But Dr. Pressly is also proud of the present: "We've had some top-notch people who came out of that school," he recalls. "People like Senator Howard Baker (the Tennesseean who became Reagan's chief of staff) and Pat Robertson."

Dr. Pressly taught Pat's English class and remembers the boy as "exceptionally good. He had a way with words and was an excellent writer. Pat was a good football player, too."

Upon graduation, Pat returned to Washington and

Lee — called "W&L" locally. There, "he was the only student I knew who could party all night and still make straight A's," recalls a former classmate. He became a Phi Beta Kappa — an honor student.

"Pat was in the Sigma Alpha Epsilon fraternity, and I was a Delta Tau Delta, but I'd see him all the time," remembers Glasgow.

"He was a great party boy. And he had a way with the girls. They all loved him."

W&L was, like VMI, an all-male school.

"But that didn't make any difference," said Glasgow. "We were within 60 miles of about five girls' schools. We'd hit all of them and Pat was always right there with us."

Two they were especially fond of were Randolph-Macon, over in Lynchburg, and Sweet Briar, not far down the road.

"The fancy-dress ball at W&L was the biggest social event of the year," said Glasgow. "We had a semester system which finished at the end of January. Then we'd always have a three-day dance series.

"One night out of the three you'd have a theme party. All those costumes came from some outfit in Philadelphia. The other two nights you just dressed up in tuxedos.

"Pat was dating this girl he had met. She was from up around Baltimore. And I had a date with a Baltimore gal, too. About the first of February 1947 we had those two girls coming down for the big dance. We were going to pick them up in Lynchburg.

"So we were going to drive over to Lynchburg to bring them back to campus for the weekend. But it just so happened that starting that Wednesday night, we got a snowstorm," he recalls. "And I guarantee you, it snowed 24 inches in 24 hours.

"But we thought, 'What the heck, we've got girls over there in Lynchburg. Let's get them.'

"So we borrowed a car from one of Pat's fraternity brothers, put some tire chains on it and went across the Blue Ridge Mountains. It was really a good-size mountain we had to climb, but we finally got over there and picked up our two dates and a couple of other girls for some friends of ours.

"It took us about three hours to go 45 miles, but the way Pat figured, it would have been better to spend the weekend with them in a ditch than to know they were over there and we were over here," said Glasgow. "I don't think I'll ever forget that weekend."

Pat had another reputation, not as a ladies' man or academician, but as an athlete.

Fraternity brother Charlie McDowell recalls one wrestling match in a column he writes for the *Richmond Times-Dispatch*. He and Pat have been pals since the age of four.

"Some of us talked Pat into going into the heavy-weight division of the intramural wrestling match," he said. "I can't remember how Pat wound up in the finals. I think there weren't enough entries and Pat drew a bye. Something like that. But there he was in the big match.

"He was up against the best athlete at W&L of his day. It was a fellow named Bryan Bell, who was an all-Southern Conference fullback and a superb defensive back."

Bell later was signed by the Detroit Lions pro football team. "In any case, the notion of how this 215-pound physical specimen would destroy a smaller, pudgy Pat Robertson was the talk of the campus."

As McDowell describes it, "Pat was a mild and jolly person and Bryan was a tough — really tough — character.

"The event drew a huge crowd for an intramural match because it was going to be so devastating. Everybody just knew Pat was going to be destroyed.

"The minute the match started, Bell came out of his corner and headed straight for Robertson. Pat went into what looked like a leaning crouch — probably terrified.

"I remember that Bell tackled him just above the knees, knocked him to the mat, and landed on him. It was all in the same momentum. Then he went into some kind of a half nelson to roll him over," McDowell said.

"But he rolled him over so vigorously that Pat came out on top. It was as if he put so much energy and movement into it that it went beyond what Bell had in mind. Pat stayed on top and pinned him within 40 seconds. It was awesome!

"I'm not sure Pat knew what he was doing, but I would say that he took advantage of a fellow who had too much enthusiasm."

Pat became the heavyweight champion.

Earlier, he had tried boxing. In the Golden Gloves he'd fought at 185 pounds in the novice heavyweight division.

"I got a technical knock-out in the semi-finals because my opponent was out of shape," Robertson remembers. "I hit him once in the stomach and he began to get sick. But I lost in the finals."

He graduated from Washington and Lee in 1950 with honors — magna cum laude. His education also included graduate study at the University of London.

Then Pat began a two-year tour of duty as a lieutenant in the Marine Corps. His assignment with the First Marine Division Forward as an assistant adjutant was to become a matter of controversy.

Then Pat decided to return to school.

"When I heard that Pat was headed for the Yale Law School, I wasn't surprised," said a college friend. "It was only natural since his father began as an attorney."

In the classroom at Yale, he specialized in tax law, but his social life had not changed from the days at Washington and Lee.

Law school buddies remember him as a good-looking, fun-loving guy who had a weakness for all-night poker games.

One party at Yale, however, changed his life. A group on campus known as "The Little People" — for students less than five feet tall — threw a party and invited ordinary-sized students from the nursing school and the law school.

Pat dropped by.

So did a nursing student from Columbus, Ohio,

Adelia "Dede" Elmer. As she remembers the social, "There was this very short person and he was following me around a little too closely. I was desperately trying to get away, so I told him I had to help out with the food."

She went downstairs and tried to look busy at the refreshment table, but when she leaned over the candles, something horribly embarrassing happened.

Her hair caught on fire.

Hardly before she realized what had happened, "a tall man with bushy eyebrows was putting it out." She remembers him clapping his hands above her head.

And that is how Pat Robertson met his wife-to-be.

His rescue made quite an impression. "I think that's probably what attracted me to him. From that point on I knew my life would never be dull."

Dede was born December 3, 1927, in Columbus, Ohio, to middle-aged parents. Her mother's late pregnancy with Dede has been described as "unexpected."

The girl was raised in an upper-crust neighborhood where social status was important. She attended private schools and attended Ohio State University in Columbus before going on to Yale.

Like Pat, she sought the fun life. She was known as a popular sorority girl and was a finalist in the Miss Ohio State University pageant.

"I was a party girl," she once told a reporter. "I liked to have a good time. We weren't religious as I know it today.

"Back then, I thought we were. I was brought up Catholic and we went to church." And she recalled, "We were straight-line Taft Republicans. This was mid-America."

When she graduated from OSU with a degree in Social Administration, her friends expected her to do what they had planned — find a husband, settle down and raise children.

But that was not for Dede. Instead she applied to the Yale School of Nursing and was accepted to the master's degree program.

"It probably was the only thing I ever did that was

different than what was expected," she says. "Nursing wasn't the sort of thing one did who had my background. They became a teacher, or a social worker, or maybe a buyer at a store. Something like that.

"But I had a strong urge to help people," she recalls. "When I started working as a volunteer at the Red Cross before I went to nursing school, I liked that more than dating."

Pursuing a nursing degree "was something I always felt I wanted to do."

Upon meeting Pat, however, things changed. Before too long, she and Pat were fanning the flames of romance.

But there was one problem.

Pat was a Baptist and Dede was a Catholic.

Neither set of parents was excited about the prospect of marriage.

Pat and Dede, however, believed it would work. Without their parents' knowledge, they were secretly married in the spring of 1954.

"We didn't bother telling anyone because neither family thought much of the relationship anyway, especially Pat's mother," Dede said. "I don't think she ever accepted it."

It was quite a while later that Dede finally told her folks when she went back to Columbus for a visit. When asked what they said, she replied, "Not much. I was pregnant."

She and Pat named their first son "Timothy."

Even before graduating from Yale Law School, Pat was becoming restless about his future. He had a beautiful wife and a fine son, but nothing seemed to be making sense.

As he wrote in *Shout It From the Housetops,* "... even in marriage I was so burdened with the futility of life."

His degree from the prestigious Ivy League school was a sure-fire ticket to success, but his life seemed to be going backward, not forward.

"After graduation," said Pat, "I had taken the New

York bar exam, but my heart was not in it, and I failed. My father was heartbroken."

He recalled his concerned father saying, "Pat, you've always made your mark; there's been nothing out of your reach. Now you fail the bar exam. What's wrong?"

Of his feelings at the time, Pat said, "I doubted seriously if I could ever explain to Dad the disillusionment I felt about life. I had tried pleasure, philosophy. Nothing satisfied. I lived with a nagging feeling that I didn't belong anywhere. Life was empty."

Pat turned to the world of business, believing he could make his mark by climbing the corporate ladder. He joined the firm of W.R. Grace & Co., where he was a financial analyst.

It was not long until he became bored. He felt life held something else and he needed to find it quickly.

Recalls Dede, "I was taking care of our son Tim and fairly contented with our life. There was this restlessness in Pat, but I thought this was pretty much how our life was going to be."

With William Riley, one of his old law school pals, and another partner, Pat set up an electronics components business. They were going to market a collapsible electronic speaker. The idea of building a huge company fast was exciting at first, but it soon lost its attraction.

Pat had joined the local Southern Baptist church when he was a boy. "But," as he recalls, "the experiences had been primarily social, not spiritual." And when he left home, he got away from attending church.

But he couldn't get away from the influence.

His mother was relentless.

Every time she wrote or called, there was a spiritual message of some kind or another.

Said Pat, "Dede felt she was a religious fanatic and I tossed the letters aside."

One night after Dede put Tim in his little bed, Pat startled her, saying that he felt he should go into the ministry. She didn't even respond. Pat finally asked, "Well? What do you think?"

"I think it might be fun." said Dede. "Maybe you could get a nice church and I could sit behind a beautiful tea service and entertain. We could have a big old manse with rooms to spare. It sounds exciting."

To Pat it seemed like a logical decision. He could make a positive contribution to a world that needed help. As Robertson said it, "And what better way to help people, I thought, than being a minister?"

Pat and Dede began visiting some churches in the neighborhood — a Moravian church, then an Evangelical Free church. For Dede, who was raised to attend Mass, it was a rather new experience.

It was during this time that Pat, who was looking for answers, turned to the Bible. Pat shocked one of his business partners one day by telling him he was going to get out of the company and go into the ministry.

"You're kidding," his partner said. "What for?"

"I don't know," Pat responded, "I just have a feeling I should do something good for mankind."

His partner could not understand. "You mean you're going to become a priest or something? What about your booze? Your salty language? And those cigars?"

Pat smiled, "I didn't say I was going to resign from the human race. But somebody's got to help this world out of the mess it's in, and I don't see where I'm making much of a contribution peddling electronic devices."

But Robertson knew that if he pulled out of the partnership and asked for his modest investment back, the business would be bankrupt. Pat knew he would have to solve this problem before he could begin the new path he had chosen.

A few weeks later, in April 1956, Pat went to Lexington to tell his mother the great news. He knew how excited she would be with his decision.

He was shocked at her response. "Pat," she said, "something's wrong. I don't think you have the slightest idea what you're talking about."

Her words were like a slap in his face.

"The pulpits of our nation are filled with men just like you. They want to do good for mankind. They want to help people, but they're doing it in their own power, and that's worse than nothing."

The faith of Pat's mother was more than religion. Anyone who really knew her recognized the fact. And what she told him that day she meant with every fiber of her being.

She sat across the kitchen table and said to her son, "How can you go into the ministry until you know Jesus Christ? You know how I know you don't know him? Because you don't talk right. You never mention his name."

Gladys Robertson went on. "You've got to accept him as Lord of your life.

"Pat, unless you do, you're going to be just as spiritually empty a minister as you are a businessman. You cannot fill your emptiness by trying to do the work of God. It's like trying to fill a bottomless bucket."

And then she looked him right in his eyes and said, "You need to be born again."

The next day Pat went back to New York.

Deep down he knew his mother was right.

For him to enter the ministry would be a sham. He also knew that the experience his mother was talking about was not really his.

One week later, he received a phone call from a Dutchman named Corneilius Vanderbreggen who asked Pat to meet him in a Philadelphia restaurant for dinner.

It is impossible to understand Marion Gordon Robertson today without comprehending what happened to him at that posh eating establishment in the City of Brotherly Love.

Pat was impressed when the gentleman told him, "God is generous, not stingy. He wants you to have the best. Order anything you want."

Corneilius was a distinguished man, immaculately dressed. He was also something called a missionary-evangelist.

Pat knew it was going to be an unusual evening when the head waiter came to the table.

As the waiter was about to take the order, Pat's host pulled a small pamphlet from his coat pocket and handed it to the waiter, "My name is Corneilius Vanderbreggen. Here's a little booklet I've written, and I want you to have it."

"Beads of perspiration were popping out of my fore-head," Robertson remembers. "What had I gotten into? Was my mother to blame for this? I had never had any contact with 'religious' people who did crazy things like handing out tracts in restaurants."

The next thing Pat knew, Corneilius pushed back the beautiful table service and laid a huge Bible in front of him. And he began to read it out loud. When Robertson remembers that night, he says, "I knew I had no choice but to sit there and act like I was listening.

"I could feel the moisture in the palms of my hands now, and little rivulets of perspiration running down my face."

He tried to smile, but couldn't do it.

He felt that every eye in the restaurant was on him.

He couldn't bear to look.

Then, while Corneilius continued to read out loud, the waiter interrupted and said, "Sir, there is a lady over at the other table who is wondering what you are discussing. I gave her the little booklet you gave me. Can you give me another one?"

"Certainly," he said. "By the way, have you ever had a personal experience with Jesus Christ?" They had a little conversation that ended with the Dutchman quoting a verse of scripture.

Corneilius gave the waiter his card and suggested he give him a call.

Pat could not believe what was happening.

All he knew was that the verse that had been quoted to the waiter was the same one his own mother had quoted. The words of Jesus, saying, "No man cometh to the Father but by me."

He immediately opened up to Vanderbreggen and told him what was happening in his life.

Pat shared how he had begun to read the Bible and how it seemed that God was talking to him through its pages.

Pat continued, "I'm convinced that God is the only hope for the world. In fact, I've decided to enter the ministry. My only problem is how to get out of business without losing everything I've got."

Corneilius didn't talk about the business. Instead, he bluntly asked Pat, "What do you believe about God?"

Robertson was getting nervous again as he answered, "I believe he is the source of all power, the guiding intellect of the universe. Not only that, but I believe he has a destiny for each man's life, and that none of us will ever be happy or productive unless we are in the center of his will."

Vanderbreggen's response surprised Robertson. "Pat, any Mohammedan could have told me what you just said. Isn't there something more?"

As Pat recalls it, "Suddenly I was oblivious to the surroundings. 'Yes, there is something else. I believe Jesus Christ died for the sins of the whole world.'" Then he added, "... and for my sins, too."

Says Pat, "I don't think Corneilius actually realized all that was taking place inside me at that moment." As he describes it, "God turned on a light within me. All my experiences with God so far had been religious, not spiritual."

Vanderbreggen paid for the expensive dinner and walked Pat across the street to the train station. Before Robertson left, Corneilius said something to Pat that he would never forget. "God wants you to walk by faith and not by sight."

He couldn't wait to tell Dede what had happened in Philadelphia. As she recently recalled it, she only had two words to say on the matter: "So what?"

She says, "I had no idea what he was telling me at the time. I thought he was telling me that we would be going to church more regularly."

But something dramatic had happened to Pat.

He walked over to the cabinet in the kitchen and started uncapping liquor bottles and pouring the contents down the drain — "expensive liquor," says Dede. "That's when I knew it was pretty serious."

Then down came the print of a Modigliani nude from the fireplace.

Dede did not understand. "I don't mind your going into the ministry, but all this 'saved' stuff is too much for me.

"If you think I'm going to put up with this the rest of my life, you've got another think coming. I'll go back to Ohio. I want my children to grow up in a normal home."

Pat's behavior changed. No more foul language.

He gave up the cigars.

He stopped hitting the bars with his partners after work. Says Robertson, "I also began devouring my Bible morning, noon and night. I read it at meals. I read it aloud to Dede after we went to bed.

"Often she just turned over and went to sleep, but I read until I couldn't see anymore."

Pat had a liberal arts education. He had studied Shakespeare. He specialized in economics. He understood politics and he knew the law.

Now he was absorbed in something he felt was completing his education and preparing him for something very special.

But what should he do about the business? The three partners had borrowed $6,000 to get it started. He couldn't ask for $2,000 and walk out.

Not long after, a man from Seattle flew in to look at a product they had advertised and got so excited about it he bought Pat's share of the business.

At last Robertson was a free man.

Free, that is, unless you consider that he was a man without a job. And his wife was threatening to take his son and go home to mother.

He knew he was free. And he knew that in September he would enter a seminary somewhere.

He was getting ready for a new race.

The boy from Lexington was getting faster on his feet.

5

Broke in Brooklyn

"I'm a nurse. I recognize schizoid tendencies when I see them and I think you're sick." That was Dede's reaction to Pat's unquenchable thirst for things that were spiritual.

But things were only to get worse.

For example, there was the time that — although they barely had a cent to their name — he decided to spend a part of the summer at a remote Canadian island, so as to get closer to God.

Or the time he sold all their possessions while she was out of town and gave the proceeds to charity. Dede was hysterical when she found out. She hid her remaining belongings at her mother's home.

Then there was the time that Pat decided that the family should move into a squalid New York City brownstone with the poor, the insane and the afflicted. Regular dinner guests included the retired madam of a nearby bawdy house.

And, of course, there was the time that he decided that he should buy his own television station from a used car dealer.

But Pat's enthusiasm for things of God was unending. It was as if a switch had been suddenly turned on inside him.

As one friend said, "If ever you saw someone make a 180-degree turn, it was Pat."

In the summer of 1956, Dede was pregnant. Suddenly Pat decided to leave her for a month to attend Campus in the Woods, the Inter-Varsity Fellowship summer camp at Lake of Bays, Canada.

The heat was sweltering, her husband was gone and she had little money for even the barest essentials. Dede was bewildered, frustrated and increasingly bitter. "I felt I was already religious and had a relationship with God," recalls the former debutante. "I didn't think he wanted me to live like this."

Why would Pat disappear like that?

With the total change that had taken place in his life, he felt he needed to get alone and find some answers. The rustic camp was located on an island, in the middle of a lake.

Every day, Pat absorbed Bible study as if he were preparing for a college exam.

There Pat was asked to deliver his first sermon at a little country church that needed a guest speaker. He took his text from the book of Daniel and titled his discourse *Weighed in the Balances and Found Wanting*. Little did the rural congregation realize that many of Pat's anecdotes about empty living were autobiographical. He was talking about his own need when he recalled what it means to have God missing in one's life.

When Pat arrived back at their little Staten Island house, Dede was so glad to see him she forgot they were broke and she was due for delivery in about two weeks. She was just delighted to have him back.

There was not much time to take a serious job before enrolling in a seminary in September, so Pat took a volunteer position at a small religious magazine, *Faith at Work*.

His office was in the heart of Manhattan.

It was a great learning experience, but it did not buy the groceries. Dede's mother came to visit a few days later.

She wanted to be there when the baby came.

Pat vividly recalled those days. "She never had liked me, having felt that Dede should have married a Catholic — a wealthy one. Quite understandably my recent actions had only reinforced her opinion that I was an irresponsible, selfish brute who was more interested in myself than her precious daughter."

When she found out Pat had returned only to work *gratis* at a Christian monthly, she flew into a rage. "I don't believe it! A Phi Beta Kappa with a law degree volunteering his services to a religious magazine?"

She went on, "I don't care if you are the son of a senator, I think you've turned into some kind of a religious oddball, and if Dede had any sense, she'd come home with me and leave you for good. Imagine! A man with two children and two degrees working for nothing. It's ridiculous!"

The baby, Elizabeth, was born August 1956.

Two weeks later, Pat enrolled at New York Theological Seminary, a three-year course of study in downtown Manhattan. And they found a $65-a-month apartment in Queens.

Immediately, Pat met several students who were seeking direction for their lives, as he was — people such as Lois Ostensen, who became assistant to Dr. Harold John Ockenga at Park Street Church in Boston; Gene Peterson, who later pastored the Presbyterian Church at White Plains, New York; and Dick Simmons, a student whose total reliance on faith became one of Pat's great inspirations.

Unconsciously Pat began building a network of people that was to continue to reappear at significant points in his future.

He was invited to the Presidential Prayer Breakfast in Washington, D.C., and was asked to speak to the Senate prayer group his father attended. There he met Robert Walker, editor of *Christian Life* magazine. When Pat returned to New York, he met Harald Bredesen, who at that time was public relations director for the Gospel Association for the Blind, but soon accepted the pastorate of the historic First Reformed Church in Mount Vernon, New York.

Pat became his associate minister.

Money was tight, hard for the young Robertsons, but both Dede remember those days

as good times. Boyhood playmate Buddy Glasgow recalls, "I remember seeing him when he came home. He
came to a party at our house at Christmastime. I was
working for Texaco out in Indiana. I came home with my
wife. Pat and his wife were there, and Eddie Gaines.

"I could see right off there was a big change in him.
Here he was.

"No money.

"Working part time at a little church and going to
seminary.

"But, you know, he was the happiest man in the
world. I'd never seen anybody so happy."

He remembers Pat telling him, "Money doesn't mean
anything to me. I know where I'm going and I'm sure
I'm going to get there."

Said Glasgow, "Pat said it. Just like that. And we all
just marveled. I told him, 'Pat, I wish I had what you've
got! Because I think you're lucky. I've got a pretty good
job and I work. But you've got something money can't
buy.' ".

Gaines, who grew up with Pat and later taught at the
University of Arizona, wasn't surprised. "I think Pat always, or at least from prep school on, had the idea of
some time becoming a minister. His mother had always
wanted one of her sons to be a minister."

The following summer, Dede went with Pat to a
Word of Life camp, in Scroon Lake, New York. There,
she made the same commitment Pat had made at the restaurant in Philadelphia. She realized that although she
had been raised as a Catholic, she had never made a total
commitment to Jesus.

Pat interviewed to become a missionary, but it did
not work

Then, he was asked to become the pastor of a large
church in New York City's upper east side. He turned it
down, and when they increased the financial offer, he
turned it down again.

He didn't feel

Just one month to the congregation.
he spoke at the Class his graduation from seminary,
nue Presbyterian Church in

Brooklyn, in one of the worst slums in America. The pulpit committee asked if he would come serve as their pastor. Pat wanted to, but something inside kept saying, "No." He recommended his friend Dick Simmons, who accepted.

Then, in June of 1959, at the age of 29, Pat Robertson graduated from seminary with a master's degree in divinity. And his family continued to grow. With the arrival of baby Gordon, the Robertsons had three children born in just over three years. Pat's future, however, was anything but clear.

His resume looked impressive but rather unusual. There were not many seminary graduates with a law degree from Yale.

It was just three weeks after graduation that Dede received a call from Ohio that her brother was to undergo a kidney operation in Columbus.

She went to be with him. While she and the children were gone, Pat felt impressed to put into practice a verse in the Bible that seemed to leap right off the page when he read it: "Sell all you have and give alms ..."

He wrote Dede and asked her to look up the verse. He gave her the chapter and number. She replied, "Honey, you do whatever the Lord tells you to do."

Pat immediately put an ad in the paper and sold nearly everything. As he told an audience later, "I didn't have that many possessions, so it wasn't all that hard."

About the only things that Pat didn't sell were a baby bed, Dede's clothes, a few pots and pans, some silver wedding gifts, and their old DeSoto car. He moved into the Dick and Barbara Simmons home in the middle of the Brooklyn slums.

Said Pat, "I gave some of the money I received from selling the furniture to Bob Pierce, director of World Vision, to help with his orphanages in Korea." The rest he gave to Simmons to help desperate families living in the streets.

To Pat, what he had done was not an idle gesture. He had sold all. He had given to the poor. He was now ready to see what his God could do with nothing .

When Dede phoned Pat that weekend, the operator told her the phone was disconnected and gave her a forwarding number.

It was the Simmonses'.

"Where's Pat?" Dede asked Barbara.

"He's here," she replied.

When Pat came to the phone he found that Dede had no idea what was going on. "I sold the furniture," he told her. "Didn't you read my letter?"

Dede was hysterical. She had not bothered to look up the references from the Bible. "I never look up verses that people scribble down like that."

When she learned Pat had not only sold the furniture, but also had given away the proceeds, she began to cry. "Pat, I just can't take it anymore. What can we do now?" she sobbed.

All Pat could tell her was that he felt he should go home to Lexington and tell his family the marvelous things that had been happening.

To Dede, things were not marvelous.

When he picked her up in Columbus for the drive to Lexington, there was not much to talk about. Dede left some of her personal belongings at her parents' home — just to be safe.

But Pat had a calm assurance that every action he had taken was for a definite purpose. They had not been in Lexington long until the phone rang. It was the local Bible Presbyterian church asking if Pat would speak there on Sunday. As Pat recalled, "The Sunday evening service at the church was followed by a radio program" on station WREL.

Several men in the church were excited about the message. They offered to sponsor him all week long on a local radio broadcast.

Pat had never spoken on the radio before.

After the program on Monday, he drove to his parents' home. His mother handed him a letter. "This came this afternoon. I thought you might be interested in it," she said.

The letter was from George Lauderdale. Pat had

gone to school with him 16 years before. Now he was pastor of a Reformed Presbyterian church in Norfolk.

At the bottom of Lauderdale's letter was a postscript: "There is a television station in Portsmouth, Virginia, that has gone defunct and is on the market. Would Pat be interested in claiming it for the Lord?"

George had no idea Pat would be in Lexington when the letter arrived. Two days later, when he felt impressed to drive the 240 miles from Norfolk to Lexington, he had no idea he would bump into Pat.

"I just happened to run into George in front of the post office downtown, and we drove up to the station together," Pat recalls.

Years later when they were discussing it, Pat told George, "The timing was unbelievable. I had come from New York City and you came from Norfolk. And here we intersected on the street in Lexington. I hadn't seen you in years."

After Robertson delivered his daily radio address, they went for a cup of coffee at the local drugstore to talk about the Portsmouth television station.

Lauderdale knew about the station firsthand. "I did the last program before it went off the air. We didn't know it at the time, but when they shut the lights off, that was it. The station just never came back on."

The Portsmouth station was owned by Tim Bright, a local car dealer. As George described it, "The place looked like a good tax deduction. He sold automobiles. When the sailors came to town they needed a car quick. He would advertise them on TV. It was quite a scene over there."

Channel 27 showed a lot of old movies, had a few local country music shows, and sold a few of Bright's cars. George recalls, "When he said, 'Lauderdale, do you want to buy this station?' I thought it was a joke. But he meant it. I said, 'No, but I have a friend who might pull it off.' "

That is when George wrote the letter.

The idea of a television station was foreign to Robertson. He didn't even own a television set.

Pat wanted to know how much it would cost to build a station like that. "Oh, between $250,000 and $300,000," said George. "But it will sell for much less than that."

Later that evening, Pat walked over to a field where he used to play football with Glasgow. He looked up and prayed. He not only felt impressed that he should buy the station, but felt that the exact amount of $37,000 was what he should offer for it.

When he told Dede, she just shook her head. It was almost more than she could comprehend. She said, "We don't have a dime. We're living like gypsies."

Pat wrote Tim Bright the next morning. "How much do you want for the station?"

Bright's answer was in the mail before Pat was to return to Brooklyn. He wrote, "For the equipment, building, and land I want $50,000. For the equipment alone I want $25,000."

Pat got excited because his figure of $37,000 was right in the middle.

But what difference did it make?

Pat was broke.

It might just as well have been $37 million.

Pat and Dede loaded the family into the car for the trip back to New York.

Dede knew exactly where she was headed and it was not a pleasant thought. She had visited the brownstone on Classan Avenue right after the Simmonses had moved in. It was "the filthiest, ugliest, most germ-infested place I've ever been in," she remembers.

The Robertsons' new home was actually a room and a half in someone else's parsonage. But considering their worldly possessions, they didn't need much room.

The neighborhood was the picture of poverty and crime. Filthy mattresses rotting at the curb. Broken bottles on the sidewalks.

Shattered windows.

Dented cars with no hubcaps. A mixture of poor blacks, Hispanics and whites living amid welfare and robbery.

Simmons remembered those days. "We were putting into practice everything we believed in."

Why shouldn't they be willing to live among the poor? It was what they had been "called" to. They had been exposed to it at seminary. And they had heard a hundred firsthand stories of missionaries who had literally given up everything to serve mankind.

But there were others besides the Simmons and Robertson families living in the messy manse. It had become home to an unforgettable collection of humanity. From mental cases to spastics, they were welcome.

Mealtime was always a surprise because Simmons had such a heart for people in need. The fare, however, was Spartan. Soybeans, being cheap and nutritious, were often the main course. They tried everything from soybean soup to soybean souffle.

It was agreed that Simmons was in charge totally. After all, he was the pastor, and that seemed to be the only way such an unusual household could be run.

Dede, however, balked at having a non-family member as an authority figure. And her Irish temper often flared. The news that Dede's mother was coming through New York on her way home from Europe was almost too much to handle.

Pat's mother-in-law, Mrs. Elmer, had seen their less-than-adequate living conditions in the past, but nothing like this. Pat and Dede felt they had reason to be concerned.

Although everyone in the household tried to make the evening pleasant, Mrs. Elmer was not the least bit impressed.

"Dede," she said, "I'm leaving in the morning for Columbus, and I want you and the children to come with me. There's no sense in your staying in this squalor."

Many years later, Dede, speaking to a meeting of a group called "Women's Aglow" in Chesapeake, Virginia, told them, "I had always been a Daddy's girl. Whatever I wanted — as long as it was within reason — I got."

So Mrs. Elmer was astonished at the desolation in which she found her pampered little girl living.

"It was a commune," Dede remembers, "and I wasn't meant to live in a commune. I don't like sharing my husband and children with anyone else.

"I had to learn to live with rats, mice, roaches and even bedbugs. When my mother came to visit, I made soybean meatloaf because all we could afford to eat was soybeans.

"At the dinner table we had a crazy man and a spastic couple who lived with us, and an ex-madam from the house next door who was saved, but still looked like a madam.

"My mother pulled me aside and said there was no reason for me to live like that — that I should come home with the children and let Daddy take care of everything."

Dede said, "I was really tempted ... but I realized that if I left Pat, I would never be happy."

What she told her mother that night in the decay of that Brooklyn kitchen even shocked Pat.

As Robertson recalls it:

"I felt my stomach tighten as I waited for Dede's answer. She spoke gently but firmly.

" 'Mother,' she said, 'for the first time in my life I realize if I leave Pat, I would not only be leaving my husband, but leaving the Lord. God is more important to me than anything else in the world and I cannot turn my back on him.' "

Her mother left.

For Pat and Dede that evening was a milestone. Whatever the future held, they were going to face it together.

But what about the television station in Portsmouth? Pat could not get it out of his mind, but the idea seemed so preposterous.

After all, there had never been a religious television station established anywhere in the world. And even though Robertson had an extremely broad education, it had not included the broadcast media.

Then there was the question of money. The station was broke and so was he. Still, to take it over, someone had to pay off the debts. But as Robertson was now in the habit of doing, before making a major decision, he needed to get alone.This was no ordinary decision. It called for drastic action.

The next morning, as Robertson tells it, "I took seven cans of fruit juice and a sleeping bag, told Dede I was not to be disturbed for any reason short of the death of one of the children, and secluded myself in the Classan Avenue Presbyterian Church next door."

For the next seven days and nights he paced the floor, read his Bible and prayed. At the end of the seventh day, he walked out of the gloomy sanctuary and announced his decision.

The answer was, "Yes!"

Immediately, he called Lauderdale to tell him the news. As George recalls it, "Pat was excited. He was coming down, but needed a place to stay." Lauderdale told him about a retired nurse, a Mrs. Mayo, that had a room in her house he felt certain she would let them use.

The next day, Pat and Dede rented a five-by-seven moving trailer and packed it with everything they owned. They hooked it to their trusty DeSoto and hugged their Classan Avenue friends farewell.

Pat, with $70 in his pocket, loaded his family into the car and headed south.

Thanksgiving Day 1959 was worth celebrating. After a brief stay with Mrs. Mayo, Pat and Dede rented an unfurnished apartment. Their table that day was a trunk with a cloth draped over it. With the Lauderdales, they sat on the floor and had their dinner. Says George, "It was one of the best Thanksgivings I can remember."

Robertson tried to get in touch with Tim Bright, owner of the defunct station, but he was out of state and couldn't be located. At this point, there had been no contact with Bright. Pat wasn't even sure if the station was still for sale.

On the Monday after Thanksgiving, Pat and Dede decided to drive across town and find the station.

It was a UHF station, Channel 27. The Federal Communications Commission had encouraged these new ultra-high frequency stations to be built in the 1950s since the TV channels 2 through 13 were nearly all spoken for. There was only one problem. Television sets sold in the United States could not bring in the signal without adding a rather expensive "converter."

Tim Bright's station had fallen, like so many other new UHF stations around the country, into bankruptcy. Advertisers won't sponsor programs unless there is an audience.

Pat had never seen a television station before and when they finally found this one, he and Dede were in shock. "I just shook my head," he said.

Channel 27 had been off the air for quite a while. It was located in a dreadful area of town on a dead-end street.

The weeds had taken over. The front door was rotting. Pat walked around to the back and found the station had been shamefully vandalized.

He climbed through a broken window and could not believe the scene.

Said Pat, "Wading through a couple of inches of broken glass and tubes, I pushed aside the debris that had been torn from the walls and let Dede in the front door."

Tubes were smashed.

Parts of the ceiling were ripped out.

Beer cans were scattered.

It smelled of human waste.

Fortunately the transmitter and the live camera had not been damaged so there was a glimmer of hope in this otherwise desolate scene.

If only they could find Tim Bright.

By this time, Pat's $70 was running out. Dede was able to get a weekend job as a nurse.

Says Lauderdale, "I was able to help Pat get a few speaking engagements at some small churches in the area."

The honorariums of $5 and $10 were enough to help with the rent. A local farmer even gave them a 70-pound bag of soybeans.

Pat became so convinced that he would get the sta-

tion that he had cards printed up with the call letters
WTFC-TV (Television For Christ). On the back he printed a list of things he wanted people to believe with him
for:

1. Wisdom to know how to buy a station.
2. God's blessing in the negotiations to buy it.
*3. Favor with the Federal Communications Com-
mission.*
4. A nationwide ministry on radio and television.

He handed the cards to everyone he met.

It wasn't until January 3, 1960, that Tim Bright returned to Portsmouth. Pat found out he was over at the
station and drove to Spratley Street as fast as he could.

He knew Robertson from the brief correspondence
they had exchanged when Pat was in Lexington. But they
had never met. Pat told him he was there to buy his TV
station.

What was the offer?

"Thirty-seven thousand dollars," said Pat, "and the
station has to be free from all debts and encumbrances."

Bright just looked at him.

He finally said, "The tower alone cost me $100,000
to build. Now you're offering me $37,000 and want me
to pay off all the debts and encumbrances ahead of time.
Is that correct?"

Pat assured him he had it right.

Then he added the kicker, "I want a six-month option."

Bright caught on right away.

Pat wanted a contract that would let him buy the station at his price anytime within the next six months.

As a businessman, Robertson was driving a hard
bargain. Pat wanted the station:
• at his price,
• less all liabilities,
• plus all the equipment,
• plus all the real estate,
• plus all the station's assets.

Bright asked, "How much earnest money are you going to give me for the option?"

Pat told him that wasn't part of the deal.

Robertson also had learned that there was a problem with the government. Bright had turned the license for the station, WTOV-TV, back to the FCC. That meant Pat might be getting a station and a transmitter, but no authority to broadcast.

There was another item.

Pat wanted to be sure the station actually worked. Bright was so convinced it would transmit a signal that he invited Pat to come back that night and see for himself.

Since the station was on the edge of a saltwater marsh, humidity had caused considerable corrosion on the parts. When Bright threw the power switch that night it sounded like a bomb had exploded.

As Pat recalled, "I jumped back as a great ball of fire burst out of the transmitter and shot up the transmission lines."

They went inside the control room and put a slide in the film chain and a record on the turntable. Bright suggested that if Pat wanted to see the station, he should go down the street and find someone who had a set with a UHF tuner on it.

Bowen's Grill was just down the block. Pat asked if they would try tuning in Channel 27 for him.

Sure enough, there was a rather weak picture, but it was there.

The audio worked, too.

That night Pat got out his old law books and drew up the option he was expecting Tim Bright to sign. He typed it on his old portable typewriter and was ready to present it the next day.

They met at an accountant's office and drove over to the station in Bright's car. He was in no mood for the deal.

In fact, he was against it. He could not understand why the son of a U.S. senator couldn't get a little financial help. "Why don't you get your dad to buy the station?" he asked.

Pat responded, "Because I am working for my Heavenly Father, not my earthly father."

The conversation immediately turned to Pat's motivation for wanting to get involved in a religious television station. As the meeting continued, Bright became more sympathetic to what Pat was trying to do.

Robertson finally asked him, "What about the option?"

Bright just couldn't sign it. But he did say, "Let me think it over for a couple of weeks."

But while he was driving Pat back to where he had left his car, Bright asked, "Pat, do I have to sign that option?"

Pat assured him there was no room for negotiation. And for all Bright knew, Pat had the money in hand and could pay him at any time. Fortunately, he never asked for a financial statement.

As they parked the car, Robertson pulled the option out of his coat pocket. Bright couldn't believe what he was doing, but he signed it.

Pat had a station. But how would he exercise the option?

Immediately, he went to work on drawing up a charter. Again, his corporate law training allowed him to file the necessary papers with the State of Virginia as a nonprofit corporation. It was filed January 11, 1960, under the name of *The Christian Broadcasting Network, Inc.*

Says Lauderdale, "In the beginning, Pat didn't even have a station, and he was already talking about a network."

The board of directors included five names:
• Harald Bredesen, the minister Pat assisted in Mount Vernon, New York;
• Bob Walker, publisher of *Christian Life* magazine in Chicago (he and Pat had become close friends since meeting in Washington, D.C.);
• George Lauderdale;
• Plus Pat and Dede.

Robertson had his charter for a network.

He had his option for a station. What he didn't have,

however, was the capital to turn the dream into reality. Nor did he have an FCC license to be broadcasting — a serious matter.

He was broke in Brooklyn and his prospects in Portsmouth did not seem much brighter.

6

$3 Network

Pat Robertson opened the envelope and cash fell out onto the table. It had only been two days since corporate papers for CBN had been filed, and in the mail here was a letter with a South Carolina postmark.

When Pat opened it, there was a note and cash.

George Lauderdale recognized the name on the note.

"The letter came from 'Jigger,' " he recalls.

Jigger?

"You see, a pastor up in our home county at the Natural Bridge Baptist Church heard I was going to be speaking in the Norfolk area," remembers Lauderdale. "He was into radio, but he told me about a television station in Portsmouth that was giving free time to preachers."

The station was none other than Channel 27, back in the pre-Robertson, used-cars-and-old-movies days.

"Once I saw the station, I knew why" they were giving away air time, Lauderdale says. "That fellow Tim Bright told me, 'Yeah, I'll give you free time. But you've got to have a singer.' "

Apparently, Bright felt nobody ought to have to listen to a sermon without also getting a little musical compensation.

A singer named Earl "Jigger" Jackson had written and asked George if he had any special meetings scheduled for him. "I told him, 'No, but I have an invitation to preach on TV if I have a singer.' " So Jigger packed his bags and drove up from South Carolina.

"The last program Tim Bright ever had on the old station was just me and Jigger," said Lauderdale. "And when they shut the station down, Jigger had to go back home."

Now, Jigger had heard what had happened to the station.

And he knew the ministry was going to need money.

Pat counted the money that fell out. One. Two. Three. Three $1 bills.

Pat told Dede, "I'm going to open up a bank account." He headed straight for the Bank of Virginia.

The clerk asked what name she should use for the new account. Pat answered, "The Christian Broadcasting Network, Inc."

When she asked, "How much do you wish to deposit?" Pat pulled out the wrinkled bills and said, "Well, we're just getting started, so my initial deposit will be $3."

By the time she charged him for the $6 checkbook, the first account of CBN was already $3 overdrawn.

"Pat's father, by this time, was getting nervous," recalls Lauderdale. "I remember once when he called me long distance. He said, 'My staff has researched this thing and it is impossible. It cannot be done.' "

But Pat was beyond the point of worrying what other people were thinking — even his own father.

The agreement with Tim Bright was that for $37,000 Robertson was to get the station debt-free. But it became clear that Pat was expected to negotiate the debts. And the station's largest obligation was to RCA, for $44,000. That was $7,000 more than Robertson had promised to pay for the whole station.

Even though Pat was demonstrating his determination and optimism, there were times when he felt like giving up.

One of those times was early in 1960 when, again, funds were exhausted. But this time it was worse. The Robertsons owed $250 in back rent and the entire family had become sick with flu. Says Pat, "I reached a stage where I was ready to quit."

He was at the point where he was even considering returning to business or law.

At his lowest point, Robertson received a phone call from a man he had met in New York, Paul Morris, pastor of the Hillside Presbyterian Church in the community of Jamaica. Morris was coming down specifically to visit Pat and his family.

Robertson won't forget that night. It was Tuesday, February 9, 1960. Morris hadn't been in the apartment five minutes when he sat down at a little desk and wrote a check for $8,000.

Pat knew that Morris did not have that kind of money. "Let's just say it was from an inheritance. And it is given without any strings attached," he said. "Use it for whatever you wish and, believe me, it makes me far happier to give it than it makes you to receive it."

To Pat, the gift was much more than money. It was a confirmation that the television project must go forward. And Pat knew where the funds were needed most.

Immediately, he began to buy a few tubes to repair the vandalism in the control room. And he put some gas in the DeSoto and headed back to New York, this time to talk to the manager of RCA's credit division.

Pat told Sam Twohig about the noble purpose of the Portsmouth station.

"That's interesting," said Twohig. "Now, what RCA wants is the $44,000 owed by Mr. Bright."

Robertson told him he didn't have that much money. The manager said RCA couldn't go lower than $25,000.

Returning to Portsmouth, Pat sent him an offer of $22,000. That was half the original amount.

RCA refused.

Then, a few weeks later, Pat sent a six-page letter telling RCA why they should donate the equipment to CBN.

RCA refused, but asked for a "reasonable offer."

Pat tried a figure of $2,500.

RCA countered with an "absolute final offer" to settle for $11,000.

Robertson sent them a check for $1,000 and went

straight to Tim Bright and offered to buy out his remaining interest for $10,000, less any accrued taxes and the cost of repairing any broken equipment.

In May 1960, Bright made a counteroffer that was even better. He told Pat, "Rather than haggle over the price, I think I will simply deed over the land, building, and tower, and all my equity in the equipment for nothing. You can take care of the debts and taxes."

The negotiations were over.

Pat could tear up the option. The Christian Broadcasting Network had received its first facilities as a gift.

And that was just the start.

A few days later, Pat received a call from the manager of a local FM radio station who wanted to know the height of the station's tower.

It was 415 feet.

"That is what I hoped," said the manager. "We need a higher tower, and rather than build one, we would like to rent space on yours."

By the time the agreement was signed, Pat had rented the tower space for $100 a month, plus when the station finished building its new studios, CBN would get the existing facilities, including all of the broadcast equipment.

The long-term lease would net $6,000 and the equipment was worth $7,000. Even though it wasn't in hand, it would certainly look good on the bottom line.

But there was still a nagging problem.

Channel 27 didn't have FCC authority to broadcast. The license was still unrenewed.

The FCC doesn't let just anyone receive a broadcast license. Pat knew he needed a commitment of at least $31,000 more to show before the government would even consider an application.

The answer wasn't long in coming. A businessman who found out Robertson needed $31,000 said, "Tell you what I'm going to do. I'll purchase your property for $31,000 and then lease it back to you for $1 a year for 20 years."

When Dede heard about it she became extremely upset. She thought Pat was making a horrible mistake. Pat might have the money, but he would no longer own the property on Spratley Street.

Nevertheless, Pat signed the contract.

Now he could fill out the FCC application.

It was the first application in FCC history stating that more than 50 percent of the programming would be religious. In November 1960, Robertson got a call from a reporter at Norfolk's *Virginian-Pilot* newspaper. "We've just received a teletype bulletin from the FCC that you've been granted a television station."

Pat was so thrilled that he told the reporter that Channel 27, renamed "WTFC" — for Television for Christ, as on the business cards printed up months earlier — would be on the air by Christmas.

He was wrong. The call letters already belonged to someone else. Robertson had to come up with something else. He proposed the letters "WYAH."

But that was hardly the worst crisis.

There would be no December debut.

Harald Bredesen was visiting the Robertsons on Thanksgiving Day. He and Pat were at the station when suddenly the man who had secured the $31,000 appeared.

He was angry. "Who put these partitions in the control room?" he bellowed.

Pat explained that they needed an audio booth and went ahead and built it. The man retorted, "If I own this building, you won't be able to place a single board without my permission."

When Pat said he just couldn't do business like that, the man threatened not to put up the money. And when Pat reminded him of the contract, he replied, "Tear it up!" And he marched out of the building.

Bredesen told Pat he should be a very thankful man.

Dede kept her peace — tactfully not recalling her strong feelings against the lease plan.

Bredesen and Robertson came to the conclusion that the businessman had never intended to put up the money. He thought Pat would go broke.

The businessman would simply take over the property when CBN fizzled. But he panicked when the FCC granted the license.

It appeared that this was his way of backing out.

Nevertheless, CBN had a broadcast license.

It also had a big debt — $10,000 to RCA.

So far, the Portsmouth experience had been a series of valleys and mountains, and now Robertson was in a very deep valley.

Dede still had a weekend nursing position bringing some money. That helped.

Then Pat was offered the position of minister of education at the Freemason Street Baptist Church in downtown Norfolk for $100 a week.

By no small coincidence, the pastor, Rev. Lumpkin, had been a minister in Lexington, and Mrs. Lumpkin had been a great influence on Pat's mother.

Pat accepted the offer.

At the same time, the Norfolk School Board, out of the blue, offered to buy the station for $35,000. There was no option, it seemed, but to present the offer to the CBN board for approval.

Robertson called Harald Bredesen and learned that he and Bob Walker would be in Washington, D.C., at a convention. Pat, Dede, and Lauderdale would meet them there.

Pat told them, "We're not just broke, we're deep in the hole." He wanted out and the school board's offer seemed a painless solution.

One by one they spoke out. Said Bredesen, "I think we should hang on to the vision and stick it out."

Walker agreed.

Lauderdale and Dede came to the same conclusion.

Pat has not been known to lose many boardroom battles, but he lost this one—fortunately, he admits now.

But something else happened at the Washington meeting. Up to that point, Pat had never really asked anyone for financial help with the project.

Board members accused him of being proud of his humility. He returned to Portsmouth with an aggressiveness people had not seen before. In a few days he printed thousands of copies of the first edition of *The Christian Viewer*.

The headline story had a dateline from Washington: "Sale of the nation's first non-commercial religious television station was narrowly averted on February 24 when the board of directors of the Christian Broadcasting Network, Inc., declined to consider sale of its Portsmouth, Virginia, station to the Tidewater, Virginia, school board.

"Talk of selling the station arose in January, following financial difficulties forced on the station when a major financial pledge was not fulfilled."

The article continued, "M.G. Robertson, president and founder, stated that the station board still feels that it is God's will to begin a religious, cultural, and educational station in Tidewater."

It was in this publication that Robertson began to share, in a low-key way, the financial picture with the people.

"Plans call for an additional outlay of $30,000," Robertson said. Of this, he explained, "$6,000 is required to complete the renovation of the plant and equipment, and $24,000 is needed to free the station from all obligations. Total cost of the station when new is estimated at $250,000. Robertson puts its present value at $90,000."

Then, in a separate article in the tabloid, Pat used logic to appeal for funds.

"Up-to-date estimates indicate that it costs approximately 1,500 percent more to minister one hour to one person in an average size church than it will cost to minister one hour to one person through WYAH-TV (the proposed new call letters).

"The normal operating budget of a church of 500 members, after gifts to foreign and domestic missions, is approximately $750 a week. For this sum, a ministry is provided to roughly 600 members in Sunday School, 350 for morning worship, and about 100 for Wednesday prayer meeting. Thus, there is a total of 1,300 worship hours at a cost of 58 cents per hour.

"It is estimated that WYAH-TV will minister to an

audience of 10,000 people for 18 hours each week. Operating budget for this time is estimated at $750 per week, thus providing a total of 18,000 effective ministry hours over television at a cost of 4 cents per hour."

Finally, in a special editorial, Robertson launched what was to become his philosophy for support. He wrote, "The sum of $30,000 is a lot of money, but not if 10,000 people gave just $3 each. If every person who reads this paper would pledge just $1 a month to the support of this station, WYAH-TV would have no financial problems."

He concluded, "The need is not for one or two wealthy men, but for many 'little people' who are faithful…"

He was no longer hinting. He was asking. The final sentence read, "Send your contributions to the Christian Broadcasting Network, Inc., Box 111, Portsmouth, Virginia."

Robertson also was establishing another theme that would eventually solidify his broad-based support. "It is our intention," he said, "to minister the gospel in a manner which accords with Holy Scripture as well as the fundamental principles underlying most of the Protestant denominations.

"We are inter-denominational in outlook, and we shall put emphasis on those things which draw together rather than those things which cause division in the Body of Christ."

The stage was being set.

The vision was being made known.

Support from the grassroots began to trickle in.

Then, Robertson decided that it was time to hire somebody to help with the project. There was one problem. He could barely support himself — much less a staffer.

He would hire me.

In June of 1961, I received a phone call from a friend, Richard Shakarian, in Los Angeles. The previous summer I had traveled with him on an overseas youth team that had conducted over 200 meetings in 27 countries. Now he wanted me to help him with the youth activities of the convention of the Full Gospel Businessmen's Fellowship International convention in Miami Beach.

It sounded good to me. I had just received my master's degree in broadcasting from Ohio State University, but had not felt impressed to accept the jobs that had been offered. I had nothing on my schedule.

En route to the Miami Beach convention, my old 1951 Buick made it as far as Tampa before it died. I sold it for junk and caught a bus the rest of the way.

There are certain dates you can never forget. For me, July 4, 1961, is one of them.

I was at the Americana Hotel and early that day someone told me about a man from Virginia who was trying to start a religious television station.

He had come to the convention with his friend, Harald Bredesen.

Since broadcasting had been my major area of study, I wanted to meet the man.

Right in the middle of a main session, a friend of mine spotted him and walked me down the aisle to where Pat was seated.

"Hi!" I greeted in a whisper. "I'm Neil Eskelin. I hear you are starting a new TV station."

"That's true," he answered, offering me his hand. "It's just marvelous what has been happening."

There, in the middle of the session, I told him about myself. About the time I finished telling him about the degree I had just completed, he offered me a job.

Well, he offered me "almost" a job.

Robertson said quietly, "Would you like to come and work with me? I can't promise you a salary, but you'll have a nice office." Then he chuckled.

I told him that I hadn't talked to him to find a job. "I just wanted to wish you the best in your new venture."

We parted company.

But later that day we met in the hotel lobby and talked again. He told me some of what had been happening in Portsmouth.

"I know this sounds impossible, but we're going to have the first religious television station in the world," said Robertson. "I'm sure I don't have to tell you about the rubbish people are being forced to watch in this country. We're going to make a change in that."

His eyes began to sparkle. "Neil, I believe that this station is going to have a tremendous impact on the entire country. There is no telling what it will lead to."

I took it all in.

On one hand, he was telling me about a station that was not even on the air.

Then he was telling me of plans to impact the nation.

"Neil, I think you can have a great role to play in what is about to happen," he said. "The opportunity we have is unlimited. It's something that has never been done before."

I didn't answer.

My mind was stirring with the possibilities.

"What do you think?" he prompted me.

I had been recruited before, but never like this. Just a few weeks earlier, recruiters from New York had been on campus. A man from NBC had offered me a handsome salary. The A.C. Nielsen Company had matched it. The offers were still waiting.

Now here was a man offering me no money, but a chance to impact America for the Lord.

"It sounds exciting," I said. "But tell me about the finances. You say you can't promise a salary? How can your staff make it?"

"Staff?" laughed Pat. "Let me tell you where we are. I have a part-time engineer and a few volunteers. You would be our first full-time employee."

Then he made another offer. "I told you that I couldn't promise you a salary, but there is something I believe I can do." Very seriously, he said, "I'll try to get you $40 a week."

I began to smile.

"What would my title be?" I asked.

Pat laughed again. "Take your pick. It's wide open. But I think you'd be perfect as the program director."

I told him I would have to think about it.

Actually, I tried not to think about it. It really was such a ridiculous offer — perhaps $2,000 a year.

Forget it!

But what I could not forget was Pat Robertson. I had never before met a man so absorbed with a cause.

His enthusiasm was contagious.

As I kept recounting our conversation, I became convinced the concept would work.

A Christian TV station.

I had no idea Pat's father was a senator, or that he had a law degree from Yale.

Not that it would have been important.

All I knew was that here was a man with a mission, a man who knew where he was going.

And he wanted me to help him.

A few days later, I borrowed $19.53 and bought a one-way train ticket to Portsmouth, Virginia.

When I arrived at the Robertsons' home, Pat wasn't surprised. "We've been looking for you," he said. "I had no doubt that you'd be here."

What a handsome family: Pat, Dede, Tim, Elizabeth, and Gordon.

But what a humble home. It was sparsely furnished and threadbare.

It was to be a Spartan experience.

But Dede was a great cook. I couldn't believe it when she told me the main dish was full of soybeans. I still remember her lectures on nutrition.

Pat and I talked until very late that night about the events that had brought him to this point. Lexington, Philadelphia, Brooklyn, Portsmouth. There was so much more to tell.

I was awake most of the night, partly because of the adventure, but mostly because Portsmouth is incredibly humid in July. Of course, the Robertsons had no air conditioning.

Television studios were not new to me, so I thought I knew what to expect. My family had traveled as a singing group and had done hundreds of TV productions from New York to Los Angeles. We'd had a daily show on WDSU-TV (NBC) in New Orleans in 1951 and 1952. We'd done a commercially sponsored series on WFLA-TV in Tampa. And I had just come from doing productions at WOSU-TV in Columbus.

But when I walked into the run-down Christian Broadcasting Network headquarters, it was like no station I had ever seen. Was it possible this facility had really been on the air?

Pat told me, "You should have seen it when we first climbed through the windows."

Robertson was proud of every piece of old equipment. But at every turn he would say, "We expect to have new turntables within a couple of weeks." Or, "We've got some new parts on order for the projector."

When he showed me where my office would be, he said, "What do you think?"

I was actually thinking about asking Pat if he could loan me $19.53 for a return train ticket to Miami Beach. But I held my tongue.

The work was totally absorbing.

There was so much to accomplish and so little time in which to do it. Pat felt impressed to set the date for sign-on October 1, 1961. It seemed totally impossible.

On Friday evening, as Pat was driving me to the house for dinner, I had my first lesson in faith. He said, "Neil, I know I promised to try to get you $40 a week, but this week has been a tough one." He handed me a $10 bill and said, "We'll make it up. Don't worry."

Worry?

It was too late.

In just those first few days, Pat's vision had inspired me. The cause was more important than cash.

On the front of the station were huge letters, WYAH-TV. The YAH was significant to Robertson — the first three letters of the Hebrew name for God, "Yahweh."

Later, the FM radio station — the one put on the air with the old equipment from the station renting tower space — would be called WXRI (the XRI stands for "Christ" in Greek).

Money, usually the lack of it, was a daily topic.

The needs were so much greater than the supply.

"I've got a fabulous idea," Pat announced as he rushed into the office. "I think I know how to raise some money and build our future audience at the same time."

He was going to buy UHF converters for $2, sell them for $6, and have some volunteers to install them. These were little "strip" converters that allow an unused channel to pick up Channel 27. We were still three years away from the time Congress would pass legislation requiring every television set to come equipped with UHF.

The project didn't pay many bills, but it got the word out that Channel 27 was getting ready to transmit a signal.

Robertson believed in CBN.

Those close to him did, too.

But there was only one word to describe the attitude in Tidewater.

Apathy.

No one seemed to care. It should not have come as a surprise. Most viewers could not receive the upcoming signal. Also, a fare of religious programming was not exactly what most people wanted. Even Christians did not act enthusiastic. People were cordial, but behind his back they were saying, "He'll never make it"; "The station won't last six months"; "Robertson has no idea what he is getting into."

To counter the criticism, Pat enlisted the help of every sympathetic community leader he could find. He would tell me, "I'm having lunch with Dr. Samuel Graham today." Graham, director of public health in Portsmouth, suddenly found himself as an active member of CBN's advisory board.

The next day it would be Walter Wilkins, president of Norfolk Motors. Pat named him chairman of the finance committee.

He involved high-profile people on committees for program policy, publicity, community relations, and more — people such as W.P. Covington, professor of dramatics at Frederick College; Robert Roughton, owner of Roughton Pontiac; George Burton, owner of a lumber company; and George VanLeeuwen, a Norfolk architect.

Robertson found pastors who would lend their names and would represent a wide variety of denominations: Rev. Joseph Buchanan, Church of the Epiphany; Rev. C.T. Mangrum, First Friends Church; Dr. Hubert Spence, Pentecostal Holiness; Rev. Edmund Berkeley, Galilee Episcopal; and Rev. Raymond Riggs, president of the Tidewater Evangelical Ministers' Association.

The credibility of the advisory board, however, did not solve other problems that would not go away. Pat was telling the world he would have the station on the air on the first day of October. But that was impossible without final FCC permission.

That notice was received on September 15.

His enthusiasm, however, was tempered by the telegram he received from RCA's credit department: "Anticipate receipt of $10,000 under contract prior to commencement of first broadcast."

Without that amount, Channel 27 could not start its signal. Robertson told me to get out a special issue of *The Christian Viewer*. In the publication, Pat wrote "We make no apology in asking you to help WYAH-TV spread the message of Christ. Pray with us that the $10,000 remaining to be paid will be met."

There was something else Pat asked for in that prebroadcast publication. It gives insight into the vision Robertson saw of the future.

He wrote, "Pray until there is a Christian network of radio and television stations broadcasting throughout this nation and even throughout the world."

To accomplish that would take an innovative approach. From the beginning, Robertson was convinced that a 100-percent diet of religious programming would not attract enough viewers to make the station viable.

We contacted every source available for free films, but the content was horrible. They were either too dull, too old, or a blatant push for some cause or product.

To make matters worse, there would be no commercial advertisers — and Pat did not want to make strong appeals for funds on television. So programming was a serious problem.

To be a broadcaster, you need something to broadcast. "Line up as many live shows as you can," said Pat.

By mid-September, we released our schedule. Robertson told the local press, "The station will begin with a broadcast day of 7 to 10 p.m., Tuesday through Saturday, 1 to 7 p.m. Sunday, and off the air on Mondays." He also said that programming would be about half-and-half filmed and live.

Also, there would be an hourly five-minute news and weather show.

For a man facing a financial crisis, Pat didn't show it. Three days before the station was to begin broadcasting, he was helping volunteers clean out an area where we planned to store props. He said, "I wish Sunday would hurry up and come. I can't wait to get on the air."

He was brimming with confidence. The rest of us, however, were nervous wrecks.

Harvey Waff, our engineer, said, "You'd better make sure you don't run two films back to back. We'll be lucky if just one projector works."

Lauderdale agreed to read the news, but we didn't have a wire service. He'd have to do rewrites from the local newspapers.

Since we had only one camera, I was trying to figure out how to change from a close-up to a wide-angle shot without the screen going blank while I switched lenses.

But more importantly:

Where was the $10,000?

The phone rang Friday night — two days before the station was to debut. The voice on the other end said, "I'm Stewart Brinsfield in Baltimore. I heard you have an FM station. I'd like to buy some air time for our church broadcast."

Pat told him the station wasn't on the air yet, but mentioned some broadcast equipment he could sell him.

"How much do you want for it?" he asked.

Pat said, "We need to raise $10,000 by Sunday, but I'll sell you the equipment for $5,000."

Brinsfield bought it on the spot but told Pat he couldn't come until Monday.

Pat took his word on it.

That was half of what Pat needed.

Saturday, the studio was crawling with volunteers. We all worked until at least 2 a.m. to get things ready for our Sunday afternoon sign-on.

Waff had run into a series of engineering problems and he announced, "There is no way we'll be on the air tomorrow. Maybe November 1, but we'll never make it tomorrow."

Dede wouldn't accept it. She kept telling Pat, "We'll make it. I just know we will."

It was Sunday and Pat had his obligations at the Baptist church in Norfolk. But all he could think about were the problems at the station.

Dr. Lumpkin knew what a red-letter day it was for Pat. He told him it would be all right for him to skip out after the Sunday school hour so he could be at the station by 1 p.m.

That morning Robertson was surrounded by well-wishers. "It seemed as though everyone in the church knew about the opening of the station," he said. Even people who couldn't receive the signal told him they would find someplace to be watching.

Pat was thrilled, but inside he was dying. Those congratulations would be meaningless if $5,000 did not show up in the next two hours.

At the studio, we were scrambling to get it all together. Waff still had tubes that wouldn't work, and the wires on the control room floor looked like a plate of spaghetti. Lines were everywhere. He said, "I've only had three hours sleep in the last two days. I never imagined we'd have so many problems."

It was about noon when Pat surveyed the scene. "What do you fellows think?" he asked.

"I know the slide projector will work, and we've got audio. But the projector is still tearing up film," I said.

About 15 minutes before we were to throw the switch, Pat paced nervously across the studio floor. As he walked back to his office, he was surprised to find Jim Coates coming in the front door of the station.

Coates was an official of the Norfolk Shipbuilding and Drydock Company and Pat trusted his judgment when it came to finances.

"Jim, we've got a problem," said Pat.

Robertson proceeded to tell him about the $5,000 dilemma. Finally, Pat asked a question he had so much difficulty in phrasing. "Do you know anyone who could lend us the money? We can't go on the air unless we have it committed."

Yes, Coates did know of a lady he thought might be able to help. He dialed the number but there was no reply.

The clock was ticking.

Pat was pacing.

Coates was thinking.

Suddenly he said, "Pat, I'll lend it to you."

A few seconds later, Pat came running through the studio shouting, "We've got the money! We've got the money! Let's get on the air!"

The $3 network was about to begin.

7

Technical Difficulties

Two hours after our announced 1 p.m. air time, WYAH-TV began beaming out a signal. The first day's programming was totally "live."

That was not the game plan, but the film projector never did cooperate.

We had one camera.

One microphone.

That was it.

I was exhausted.

We had spent all night trying to get equipment ready.

Then in the final moments the projector began shredding film and the camera started acting up.

A local church singing group, the Branch Sisters, sweltered under hot lights while we offered excuses.

Finally, two hours late, engineer Harvey Waff threw the On-The-Air switch. Since our headsets didn't work, he only got my attention by knocking on the glass of his makeshift control booth.

I focused the camera on Pat, standing on our makeshift set.

He had never appeared on television before, but when I gave him the hand signal, he began to smile.

It wasn't an ordinary smile.

It came from deep inside, the satisfied look of a man who has faced an impossible challenge — and won.

"My name is Pat Robertson. Welcome to the Christian Broadcasting Network."

As he spoke those words, America's first religious television station became a reality. After his opening remarks, we faded to a slide while the camera focused on a little sign that said "Golden Nuggets."

The Branch Sisters began to sing. The screen faded to black while the camera found them near the old upright piano.

Then, Damon Wyatt, a local Baptist minister, spoke. The screen faded to black again.

Another slide was put on the screen while we rushed everyone out of the studio so George Lauderdale could read five minutes of news.

Then, we signed off.

Pat rushed into the control room.

"I just had a call from a man in Newport News. He said we were coming in loud and clear."

That was amazing since some people two blocks away walked over to say they could hardly get a picture.

On paper, our signal looked great. Channel 27 had a maximum power of 17,400 watts. Our "Grade A" signal was to cover 11 miles. Our "Grade B" was listed for 17 miles.

In reality, however, no one was quite sure what would happen once we hit the air.

But Pat was not bogged down in such mundane questions for the moment. He was envisioning a complete TV network — and impact on America.

"I agree with FCC Chairman Minnow who calls commercial television a 'vast wasteland,' " Pat told the local newspaper. "Our job will be to transform that wasteland to the moral and spiritual benefit of our viewers."

The story ran under a small headline, "Unique Religious TV Station Airs Today."

The fact there was coverage at all was a moral victory. Earlier that week, Pat had asked me to plead with the paper one more time to print our program schedule. The editor of the entertainment section smiled and said, "We'll consider it. But I'm sure you know there aren't too many sets equipped to receive the signal."

The editor was right but we were ready to write a new chapter in the history of television programming.

Yet, it would be three more years until the government would require all television sets manufactured in the United States to be equipped with UHF.

We were breaking other ground, too. Pat has always been known to have definite opinions. When it came to how the station was to operate fiscally, he made his position clear.

"No commercials."

And that's the message Pat wanted me to underscore in the October 1961 issue of CBN's *The Christian Viewer*.

The article read, "Pat Robertson, WYAH-TV president, reiterated that the station will accept no commercial advertising of any nature. 'Our staff cannot be diverted from its primary task of ministering God's Word,' he emphasized. 'We cannot afford to use our time to service commercials, however worthwhile the products involved may be.' "

Channel 27 held a commercial FCC license — it was not a public service or educational station barred from accepting commercial messages. Thus, there was nothing to prohibit the selling of advertising ... except Pat.

He did not believe it was time to even consider airing commercials, although budget was $1,000 a week and most weeks we did not reach it.

In those lean, early days, Robertson was not only the president, he was a "hands-on" president. He had his hands on a mop when the roof leaked and his hands on the camera when no one showed up to operate it.

The old RCA TK-11 camera dominated the studio. It was mounted on a huge "dolly" that weighed a ton. And it had a four-turret lens that you had to turn by hand in order to get different effects, such as wide-angle or close-up.

There was no "zoom" permitting the operator to dramatically fill the screen with the speaker's face or to gradually pull back until viewers could see the whole studio.

And the old camera had other problems — such as "burn-in."

"Move the camera. Move the camera," Robertson

would tell the volunteer operator. That was the only way to avoid burn-in, a condition that causes the screen to show the previous picture, even when you aim at something new. The old image then slowly fades out.

The heart of the camera was a three-inch Image-Orthicon tube that Robertson was proud to say "came from NBC in New York."

Actually, they were hand-me-downs. Pat made friends with an RCA engineer in Rockefeller Center who would save the tubes NBC discarded when they reached about 1,000 hours of use. Then we would add another 1,000 hours ... and "burn in."

Newer cameras had an "orbiter" that would electronically rotate the lens to avoid the problem. Our cameramen became the orbiters as they constantly had to keep things moving.

Robertson hosted two programs every week.

"The Deep Things of God" was seen every Wednesday and Friday night at 9:45 p.m.

"The Lesson" was a 30-minute Saturday night preview of the curriculum most Sunday schools would be teaching the next morning.

As an early employee remembered, "Pat had little concept of time when he was on the air. We would give him hand signals but he got so engrossed in the topic that he'd ignore us. Since his was the last program before sign-off, no one seemed to mind."

The fact that CBN had only one camera did not stop our creativity.

Some nights on Robertson's "Deep Things" set we would place a large mirror on an angle next to Pat. When the camera would pan to the right, there would be a great profile shot.

The official opening ceremonies of WYAH-TV took place on a Wednesday night, not long after the station began telecasting.

Robertson said, "Make a special set for tonight."

We did our best with the materials at hand. We nailed four "legs" to an old door and made a table which we covered with an orange cloth but you couldn't see color on Channel 27 anyway. Pat wanted it to be a "perfect" night. Norfolk's mayor, Fred Duckworth, was there. So was Dr. Clyde Taylor, executive secretary of the Evangelical Foreign Missions Association.

The dignitaries were seated behind the makeshift table.

When Mayor Duckworth stood to make his official remarks, I said "dolly in" to the cameraman through the headsets.

It was Bill's first night as a volunteer cameraman. He grabbed the lower part of the heavy camera and began to push.

And the heavy thing wouldn't stop.

"Oh, no!" I yelled as it crashed into the table and flattened the honorable mayor against the wall.

Robertson just laughed.

There really wasn't much else to do.

When gospel singing groups would come to Tidewater, Pat would clear an hour of the evening schedule and give them a "special."

One group, the Klaudt Indian Family from Atlanta, had a record out, so we thought it would be novel to play the recording and let them just move their lips. We'd never tried that before — although it was becoming standard practice at the bigger stations.

After all, it seemed that it would be an improvement over our one-mike audio.

Rehearsal went fine. But during the live show, the audio man somehow played their 45-rpm record at 78-rpm.

Those were the fastest moving Indians you ever saw.

And they sounded more like chipmunks.

The screen faded to black. *"Please Stand By. We Are Experiencing Technical Difficulties,"* read the message filling the suddenly silent screen. That was one message we kept loaded in the control room projector. And, without doubt, we set a record for its use.

For a man trained as a lawyer, Robertson surprised the staff with his technical knowledge of broadcast engineering. More than once you could find him on the floor replacing a tube that had just blown.

And Pat also had creative ideas about how to spice up our programming. About a month before the station went on the air, Pat had called me into his office. "Neil, I know you've been busy setting up the schedule, but there is one area that looks weak. We've got to do something that will capture the attention of children."

I told him about some of the free films we had offered for kids, but he wanted a live show.

He also said, "I think you ought to host it."

Then he came up with a format. "Let's have a little stuffed bear as the star of the show. And you can talk to the bear."

I guffawed but he got excited.

"We're going to call the bear something like 'Mr. Pingo,' " he said. "And you can sing a few songs and tell a few children's stories."

A few days later, when Pat wrote a column about the station, he said, "We will be the only television station in Tidewater which will have a first-rate program for children broadcast at 7 p.m. five nights a week."

He continued, "We will be the only television station in Tidewater which will refuse to broadcast any program which will be harmful to the Christian character of your children.

"We will be the only television station in Tidewater which will place the eternal destiny of your children above ratings, above finances, in fact, above every other consideration except the will of God."

When I read it, I knew the program had better live up to its advance billing.

The next day, I visited a local funeral parlor and said, "We need some fake grass to build a set for our new children's TV show."

We draped it over a little mound so the person who would move the little bear's mouth could lie on the floor and hide behind it.

At first, Robertson wanted a "talking bear," but that meant a script, lots of rehearsals and extra talent.

We decided, instead, to put a "squeaker" in the bear's mouth. That way I could ask a question, the bear would squeak and I'd tell the kids what he said.

It also meant we could ad-lib through the whole show. They called me "Cousin Neil." I wore a cowboy hat, played the ukulele and sang to the camera and Mr. Pingo.

Another program Robertson was proud to add to the schedule was John Stallings, with his telecast in sign language. It was called "The Deaf Hear" and was seen every Tuesday night at 8 p.m. At the close of one broadcast, Harvey Waff motioned for Pat to come to the control room. There were sparks flying and smoke coming out of the audio booth. "We've just blown a tube. We're still transmitting a picture, but our sound is gone," said Waff.

Robertson ran back to the studio and tried some sign language of his own to get Stallings to stay on the air. Then, remembers Pat, "I realized he didn't understand me. So I grabbed a piece of cardboard and started writing him a big sign.

"Then it hit me. We were off the air with the sound anyway!"

So, while Stallings continued his sign language to the camera, Pat shouted, "Can you keep going until we get it fixed?"

The next day, CBN got its first nationwide news coverage. The Associated Press picked up the local newspaper article and teletyped it to most major newspapers. The *New York Daily News* headlined it, "Power Off, Deaf Hour On." The story read, "The sound failed on station WYAH-TV in Portsmouth, Va., at 8:30 last night, but the Rev. John Stallings went right on with his weekly half-hour show, 'The Deaf Hear,' in sign language.

"The minister stayed on until the station went off the air at 10, ad-libbing with his fingers the last hour."

Power failures, projector problems and transmitter malfunctions were common.

Robertson did not apologize for the poor equipment. After all, as Waff used to quip, "We have the best equipped religious television station in the country."

True, since we were the only one.

"Wow! Those fellows have powerful voices," we said as a men's trio hit the crescendo at the end of their song. Suddenly, the transmitter just "blew."

Power in the studio went dead.

The station was off the air.

We had known the trio was good but this was unbelievable. Robertson recalls, "We scurried around trying to find what had happened and finally managed to pry open the doors behind the big transformers that carried the tremendous voltage necessary to operate the transmitter. There, caught between two electrical poles, was a tiny mouse, completely fried."

Waff cut the power. Robertson reached in and pulled out the roasted rodent.

Pat ran back into the studio to tell the viewers (or what was left of them) what had happened.

Then he proceeded to apply the lesson to life, with an analogy of how small things can short-circuit the power in our lives.

It would have been great to capture shows like that on videotape but we didn't have such technological miracles in those "covered wagon" days at CBN.

We certainly couldn't afford to save the shows on film. So our efforts went out over the airwaves, into viewers' TVs — and were gone. Some shows originated on film, of course. From the first, we fulfilled Pat's vision of a half-and-half mix of religious and secular shows.

Robertson believed from the very beginning that in order to attract an audience for a religious show, we had to get their attention first.

He told me, "Find the best films available that are wholesome and entertaining. That's what we will promote."

Even on opening day, the small newspaper story about CBN's debut was accompanied by a large photo of Jim Bishop and Fran Allison on the set of their show filmed from New York, "For Your Information." As with every other film we got permission to use, it was free or we wouldn't have shown it. What was our fare for an average evening? Here is what it was like on Thursday night, October 10, 1961:

At 6:55 p.m., our test pattern came on the screen. It was useless to start earlier since we didn't have enough programs to fill the time. Plus, engineer Henry Waff had another job.

"Mr. Pingo and His Pals" came on at 7.

Thirty minutes later it was "World Adventure." That was a catch-all title for any travel film an airline or tourist bureau would loan us to promote their destination. That night it was "Tahiti, Islands Under the Wind."

The content of some of these shows made the staff nervous.

"What are we doing showing hootchy-kootchy dancers?" said one staff member.

One fellow in the film room would actually put his hand over the projector lens when the film included someone smoking or pouring an alcoholic drink.

Swear words were "bleeped" by trying to cut out the sound right on the air. It did not always work.

We tried to screen everything that came in, but most days the films would arrive in the afternoon and we'd have them on the air that night — sight unseen.

There was a five-minute newscast at 7:55 p.m., followed by "Tidewater Teens" with host Billy Wolfe at 8. It was a live production and a showcase for talented area youth.

At 8:30 we screened "Mission Safari," a half-hour film show supplied by missionary boards from several organizations.

At 9, "Project 27," hosted by Wilbur Presson, was the station's attempt to present lively discussions on current events.

It was followed at 9:30 by "Scope," a broad title for a 15-minute travel series.

The show for October 10 was "From Kitty Hawk to Calabash."

Dede Robertson had her own 10-minute show, "Lifeline," twice a week at 9:45 p.m. It addressed topics of particular interest to women. Then, just before sign-off at 10, there were five minutes of news and weather.

Robertson knew it was not a schedule that would set the world on fire. It was only a start and he understood that better than anyone else.

He ran the camera many nights during the first year of the show. Actually we should have put the camera on Pat. It was hard to believe that the president of the Christian Broadcasting Network could have produced so many antics trying to get us to laugh on the set. It usually worked.

It took a minimum of seven people, most of them volunteers, to keep a live show on the air. That is why when a minor flood covered Portsmouth roads one evening, we almost cancelled "Mr. Pingo and His Pals." Only two of us showed up.

The engineer and I.

He said, "Let's go for it."

He threw the transmitter switch and ran into the studio to grab the camera.

I played the theme song in the announcer's booth and ran out to the set.

We were stuck.

Mr. Pingo was just sitting on the grass.

There was no operator to move his "squeaker."

He just sat there motionless.

"What's the matter, Mr. Pingo? Not feeling well tonight?" I asked.

There was no response.

The show was only scheduled to run for 30 minutes, but it lasted two hours that night. No one showed up for the rest of the programs.

Just me and that silent bear.

I finally told the viewers, "If you'd like Mr. Pingo to start feeling better, why don't you write him a letter or send him a get-well card?"

Two days later, Robertson rushed into my office and said, "What's happening? Look at all of this mail. The kids are concerned about Mr. Pingo."

That is when we began to know we had an audience

out there. After that episode, the show expanded to one hour nightly.

The adventures of Mr. Pingo were amazing. One evening we sent him scuba diving. Actually, we shot the picture through a goldfish bowl while Eric AuCoin, our announcer, blew bubbles into a glass to get the perfect sound effect.

We even sent Mr. Pingo to the moon. The entire staff worked hard on this one. Our goal was to blast the bear off the earth and then lower him down to a fake moon surface in a capsule. We even had an astronaut's helmet on him.

The studio was filled with people that night. That wasn't unusual since the show was often followed by a broadcast by a local church — which would bring its entire choir.

That evening, just before the end of the show, we were ready for blast-off.

What happened next was a disaster.

The stage powder we set off was 10 times the amount we needed.

The studio was overcome with a dense fog.

Choir members coughed as they ran for the exits.

There was so much noise in the studio that I felt something had to be ad-libbed.

"I didn't think there were people on the moon," I said with a deadpan voice, "but I can sure hear them!"

Mr. Pingo squeaked.

I said, "Oh, you can hear them, too?"

As the choir began the next show, members looked as if they were singing in the clouds. It took five minutes to clear the smoke from the studio.

At Channel 27, the audience was slowly increasing, but the funds were not coming in. Some weeks, the small payroll could not be met. Pat would say, "We'll just have to catch up later."

One faithful worker, Wilbur Presson, was at the station almost every day.

He was not on the payroll but anyone would have believed he was. As with many others, he felt so strongly about what Pat was doing, he gave the station every extra hour he could find.

The Robertson home was rather small, so I moved in with the Pressons for $10 a week.

It was amazing how we stretched the little money we had. For lunch, Pat found "The Tip Toe Tea Room." It was a boarding house with all you could eat for 75 cents. Oh, it was good. We'd have Southern vegetables, chicken and dumplings and bread pudding.

The local press often talked about Robertson's father but Pat didn't. During my time at CBN, I do not recall one instance that Pat tried to gain leverage by throwing around the name of the senator.

But Pat would sometimes talk about him privately. "He just has no concept of what I'm doing down here," Pat would say. "But someday he will understand. Someday."

A few of his friends in Lexington, however, were beginning to take note. Julia Martin, for instance. She recalled, "When Pat started the station, one of my friends said, 'You just watch. Pat is really going to do something with that station.

" 'He knows the law.

" 'And he knows how the communications system works up in Washington.' "

In the spring of 1962, Robertson had a visit from his boyhood neighbor, Buddy Glasgow.

He recalls, "When Pat was first starting out in Portsmouth, I had to attend an insurance meeting in Williamsburg, so I wrote Pat and told him we would drive on over."

Pat contacted him and said, "I'd like to show you the place."

Says Glasgow, "We just marveled at how he'd gotten the funds together to build it." But the thing he remembers most was Pat saying, "One of these days you're going to turn on an Atlanta TV station and you're going to see us."

On one wall of Robertson's office was a large map of the United States. There were circles around many of ᴛhe major cities of America: New York, Chicago, Houston, Philadelphia, Indianapolis, Los Angeles, Atlanta …

Pat would talk about production centers he envisioned at key points around the United States. He would say, "Someday we're going to link up these cities by microwave or special lines." He even talked about having CBN programs on secular stations.

That, however, wasn't Pat's first media map. Even in Brooklyn, he had drawn circles on a Rand McNally.

As an executive, Pat was a strong authority figure, but he never pretended to have all the answers. For example, after he'd announce a plan of action, he would ask, "What do you think?"

If knowledge is power, Pat had it. He did not just talk; he listened.

George Lauderdale remembers the early CBN board meetings. "He was definitely not autocratic. When a topic came up, around the room it went. But once it was decided, there was no question who would get the job done.

"In fact," said George, "I was knocked off my feet by the way the meetings were run. I was expecting a cut and dried, dictatorial approach. But it just wasn't the case with Pat."

Staff meetings at CBN were not always held at Channel 27. There would be too many distractions.

I recall one meeting in particular as if it happened yesterday. About 10 of us spent a Monday afternoon in the sanctuary of the Freemason Street Baptist Church in downtown Norfolk.

We talked. We prayed.

Pat began talking about the future. "I believe we are going to be broadcasting to people all across this country. And I can see our programs being seen in Africa, Asia and South America. I see thousands, hundreds of thousands, even millions of lives being changed by what we are doing here," he said.

Then he talked about something that seemed 50 years away. He said, "I believe we are going to see satellites circling the skies, beaming our programs down to every continent. And it won't be very long."

We came away from the "retreat" with tremendous expectations for the future.

An employee who attended those meetings said, "I never had the feeling I was working for Pat Robertson. He always made me feel I was working for the cause he represented."

The mission was the message. Robertson was not only impacting lives through a transmitter. People who worked with him were affected, too.

Dan Morstad is a good example. I remember the night he walked into the station and asked if he could sweep the floor. Morstad recalls, "I had enlisted in the Navy and was assigned to the *U.S. Valcour* for a tour in the Persian Gulf. When we docked in Portsmouth, I wandered into a serviceman's center and signed up for a tour of a local television station. It was WYAH-TV."

Dan remembers, "They told us that if anyone wanted to be a station volunteer, all we had to do was show up."

He did and asked for a broom. The second night we had him running the camera.

"I watched Pat," recalls Morstad. "He had something I didn't have. And I wanted it. You could see the tremendous pressure he was under, yet he seemed so relaxed.

"I was accepted for who I was. Nobody said, 'You don't fit into our mold, or our pattern.' I guess you could call Pat an equal opportunity employer.

"For example," Morstad says, "I was a Christian, but nobody at the station talked to me about my particular faith or denomination. Pat never tried to lay a trip on me."

Morstad added, "What he had just flowed. And he's been a great example for my own life."

Today, Morstad lives in Minneapolis and runs a crisis counseling center called "Love Lines."

Willie Wilder, the station's first film editor, told me, "The cause was grand even if the money wasn't." Now employed by the United States Postal Service, Willie used to lie behind the fake grass and work Mr. Pingo's squeaker.

He still has the little bear at his home.

Funds were always tight but Robertson knew the priorities. The electric bill was always number one. Without power there would be no station.

And we all knew that Pat would often pay CBN bills out of the $100 he was getting each week from the Baptist church in Norfolk. For example, when the station couldn't write my promised check, the cash he would give me obviously came from his own pocket.

The demands of the station eventually caused a personal financial crisis for Robertson.

Then the long-awaited FM station WXRI — created from the bartered equipment Pat had gotten for renting space on the tower — came on the air.

Pat's time was stretched beyond the limit.

Live television.

Live radio.

Plus, a full-time position at the Baptist church.

One day the inevitable happened. A member of the church board was asked to tell Pat, "The committee has decided we need you full time at the church or you'll have to leave."

Pat felt he was doing a good job for the church but, deep inside he knew the committee was right.

"I was working at it," he says, "and we were having a good measure of success but my heart was in radio and television."

So Robertson wrote his resignation.

He knew the station could not pay him a salary, so he suddenly faced a bleak financial situation. But within two days, a member of the Parkview Baptist Church in Portsmouth came to the station. He was a member of the pulpit committee.

"We need a supply minister for a few months while we search for a permanent pastor," he said.

It was a large church, just a few blocks from the TV station. When Pat told him about his time constraints, he was told, "Don't worry about it." All they asked was that he show up for three church services a week. And they offered him the exact amount he had been getting — $100 a week.

Robertson served the church six months before they found a pastor. Just before his last Sunday, they allowed him to do a special mailing to the church membership, seeking support for WYAH-TV.

Fred Beasley got the mailing. His response became something the Robertson family had never expected. He asked Pat to visit him at his office.

Beasley had a rather notable reputation as a local philanthropist. He was a multimillionaire who had made his fortune in the ice and coal business.

He closed the door to his office and said, "Pat, I want to help you out."

Immediately, Robertson thought about the needs of the station. He could see new lighting being installed.

A second camera.

New tubes for the transmitter. Even air conditioning for the studio.

"No," said Beasley, "I don't mean the station, I mean you, personally."

He explained that he felt impressed to give him a salary so he would not have to take any funds from the station, and so he could give full time to building the network.

"Well," said Beasley, "how much do you need to live on?"

Understandably, Pat was in such shock, he couldn't come up with an answer. He told Beasley that he would meet him the next Monday with an answer.

When they met again, Pat told him the figure, "$100 a week."

"Are you sure that is enough?" asked his new benefactor.

Robertson assured him that he had lived on that exact amount for two years and could continue.

But Beasley had something else to offer. "We have a nice house near your TV station and we'd like for you to have it, rent-free, as long as you like."

Pat accepted but Dede just exploded when she saw the place. It wasn't exactly a slum house but it was very close. "I don't care if it is free," she said, "I think we ought to be able to live where we want." But they did move in.

For Dede, the eternal decorator, this was a monumental challenge. And considering the uncomfortable neighborhood, she made it a comfortable family home. It was disturbing, however, that a graveyard was right in back of the house.

It was two years later that Pat had an architect friend draw up a Georgian-style home. It was going to be their dream house. His idea was to find some land out in the country and somehow begin to build the project.

He finally summoned up the courage to see Beasley with the idea that he might own some land and let Pat build on it.

"It's a lousy idea," said Beasley. He said he couldn't understand why Robertson should want to build something new when "I have an empty house out in the country you could live in." He also told him the house had been boarded up for five years.

Again, Pat needed time to think about it.

And, again, Dede was opposed. "It's time we have our own house," she said.

Pat finally talked her into driving out for a look. It was on a large parcel of land that included Frederick College.

They drove on a private road through the woods, then through a pasture and straight ahead of them, there it was.

Says Pat, "We caught our breath.

"It was magnificent."

Magnolia trees. Tall, white columns across the front. Four bedrooms. A huge kitchen.

A large living room and dining room. It was right out of *Gone With the Wind*. There was even a barn where Pat could have horses.

Although they didn't have the title, it became a place of their own.

A place to raise their family.

A Southern mansion that would provide a retreat amid the battles that lay ahead.

8

"Phones Went Crazy"

"The studio looked like something put together with coat hangers. I wondered how anyone could have the audacity to think he could have a real program under these conditions!"

That is what Ben Armstrong, executive director of the National Religious Broadcasters, said about his initial visit to CBN in 1962. "Robertson had seemed like a rational person when I met him at the First Reformed Church of Mount Vernon where my friend Harald Bredesen thought he was a top-rate student assistant.

"Of course, his credentials had been impressive — not what every ministerial student had, such as a degree in law."

Armstrong also knew that Robertson had once been a partner in an electronics firm, so he knew Pat was aware the station was less than adequate.

Robertson laughed and told him, "Right now the station's signal hardly reaches around the block. That's when it works."

But Armstrong remembers Pat paraphrasing the Bible, saying, "If we are faithful with a little bit, He will trust us with more."

Robertson, in those early days, was charting new waters. He had accomplished something many people had talked about but no one else had made work. And word of a television station devoted to Christian concepts spread like wildfire throughout the evangelical community.

"I believe I am supposed to start a station in San

Francisco," one letter said. "How do I go about it? What do I do first? Can you help me?"

Letters and phone calls like that were coming in an increasing number. Robertson was not shy at spreading the UHF gospel. He was saying, "Apply for any available UHF station in your area. You have no idea how valuable it will be someday."

It was not long until he began to receive invitations to tell his story at religious conventions around the country. Christian businessmen, in particular, were beginning to see the potential. They wanted Pat to give them information. But even more, they wanted his motivation.

In Portsmouth, however, things were falling apart. All the staff was under great "financial and spiritual" pressures.

At one point, people began to take sides.

Robertson blamed himself for part of the problem. He recalled, "I was so desperate for help that I indiscriminately took anybody who came along with a Christian testimony."

The fact that CBN's pay scale was low resulted in employees feeling they were doing Robertson a favor. Said Pat, "Most of our volunteers were immature and caused more problems than they were solving."

The pressure-cooker of finances was usually boiling over. It was relentless. CBN was growing but the income was not keeping pace.

Every staff member had a solution. "Let's hire a sales team and sell advertising," said one. But Robertson was still opposed to the commercial concept.

"How about giving daily financial updates to let people know where we stand?" Pat didn't like it. He thought it was "begging in disguise."

The money question was a dilemma Robertson could not seem to solve.

"I remember when a $100 gift was like a fortune to CBN," recalls Wilbur Presson, who shared Pat's concern for finances.

After Robertson sifted through all the advice on fund raising he had been given, he suddenly was awakened to the fact that, "Dede and I had faith to see the station get on the air."

The staff, too, had to have faith that somehow enough money would come in to keep it afloat.

That is when a concept hit him that was so strong he could not understand why he had't considered it before. It was a concept that would revolutionize the struggling station on the backwaters of Portsmouth. It was surely the fuel that would launch CBN into orbit.

"Faith partners!"

That was it.

Robertson was ready to ask every viewer to be a "partner" and exercise the same faith he had and the same faith his staff had.

He would ask them to make a commitment, on faith, to support the station every month.

Hurriedly, Pat put a pencil to the budget. "We need $7,000 a month," he told the staff. The plan was to enlist 700 people to become team members, or "partners," with CBN with a pledge of $10 a month.

They, too, would take a step of faith.

The first "700 Club" telethon was held in the fall of 1963. By today's standards it was pathetic: a few phones on a makeshift set, an area for music and a spot for Robertson to show the totals.

The fundraiser only lasted a few days and it topped anything that had ever happened before. But when the final tally came in, only half of the goal of 700 "faith partners" was reached. The $3,500 a month, however, was something to build on. The "family" of CBN was growing.

Robertson was also beginning to attract some key individuals who could make a difference in programming and production.

Bill Garthwaite was a producer-director at the local CBS affiliate, WTAR-TV.

Like Pat, he became disenchanted with the glamor of the secular world. "I got to the point where the futility of what I was doing was getting to me. There was no purpose to it."

He joined CBN.

Said Bill, "What I liked about Pat was that he was a visionary but really a down-to-earth man."

Garthwaite remembers when he married his wife, Jeanie, in 1963. "Pat came over to the house in his old Marine fatigues and helped me move furniture all day. That's the kind of guy he was."

He also remembered walking into Robertson's office and seeing the organizational chart. "Here we had this tiny staff and on Pat's wall was a huge flow chart showing every division, department and function of the station," Garthwaite recalled. "You would have thought it was a major corporation."

By now Channel 27 had a full day of programming, plus, the FM station had established a niche for itself in the Tidewater market, pulling ratings that made it one of the top five stations in a 20-station market.

"We were able to do much better production on radio than we could on TV," said an early disk jockey. "And once we increased our power, the size of the audience increased dramatically."

Robertson's station, broadcasting at 50,000 watts from a 300-foot tower, became Tidewater's most powerful station. The "700 Club" telethon in the fall of 1964 increased the base of "faith partners," but it was still a day-to-day, nickel-and-dime existence.

Robertson was also becoming concerned about television programming. He desperately needed a new children's show. In June of 1962, I had left the station to begin several years of travel and speaking engagements that would take me to many countries of the world. "Mr. Pingo" was on the shelf.

During the spring of 1965, a young couple was conducting a series of meetings at a church in Tidewater pastored by Gordon Churchill. Their names — Jim and Tammy Faye Bakker.

Churchill had a part time job at Robertson's FM station. "They also have a television station over there," he told Bakker. "But they have a big problem. They have an urgent need for new programs."

Like a flash, Churchill thought about the puppet shows Tammy was doing for the children at his church. He snapped his fingers and said, "Why don't we go down to the station and talk with Bill Garthwaite. They've been looking for someone to do a children's program. Maybe you can help them."

Jim said, "Why not? I don't know anything about television, but I have worked with kids."

When they arrived at the station, Garthwaite talked with them about the need Robertson had expressed for such a program. "I'm not concerned with your lack of experience in broadcasting, Jim," he said. "I think the puppets would more than offset that. Kids are always interested in puppets."

That week, Jim and Tammy decided to give it a try. They did a live show, with Garthwaite as director. The Bakkers then left town and forgot about television. But late that summer, when the Bakkers returned to the area, Robertson had lunch with them and drove them over to the station.

Pat shared his dreams with Bakker, who also got excited. The Bakkers' kids show, *Come On Over,* went on the air in September 1965. Their audition show from a few months earlier had been easy, but now the pressure was on and when the camera came on Tammy Faye, she just froze. Jim had to rescue her.

Their set included a white frame house with a front porch, plus bleachers for the studio audience. The Bakkers knocked on doors in the neighborhood trying to fill the seats. Before long, the audience was increasing, and so was the mail.

It was Halloween that got everyone's attention. The Bakkers promoted an event at the studio and hundreds showed up. Robertson was beginning to see the power of television to influence young people.

The invoices kept arriving and the debts were piling up. By the fall of 1965, CBN was $40,000 in debt. And, for the size of the operation, that was a staggering total.

To Pat, it was a shame to have assembled such a great staff and not have the funds to continue. So he mus-

tered the courage to approach Fred Beasley again. He
wanted a loan for the $40,000. But when Pat showed
him the books, he said, "It seems to me that you're on the
verge of bankruptcy."

Beasley's advice to Robertson wasn't what he wanted but perhaps it was what he needed. "I think you ought
to sweat it out," he said kindly.

The November telethon could not come too soon for
Pat. He was counting on it to provide the escape from increasingly concerned bill collectors.

"Ten thousand dollars a month? It will never happen," whispered the pessimists on staff when Robertson
announced his goal for the 1965 "700 Club" fund raiser.

The goal was to underwrite the station's proposed
$120,000 annual budget. Pat wanted it to be positive and
upbeat. He was determined not to dwell on the $40,000
deficit. Former nightclub singer and Hollywood recording star Tony Fontaine was brought in for the event.

By the closing hour on Sunday night, the staff was
exhausted. The phones were lighting up but the total
amount raised was only $80,000. Pat knew there was no
way the station could survive without a financial blood-
letting.

Just as the telethon was about to end, an amazing
turnaround took place. One of the telethon hosts broke
down and began to weep on camera.

His voice was breaking as he sobbed, "We are on
the verge of bankruptcy and just don't have enough money to pay our bills."

Robertson recalled, "Immediately, the phone lines in
the studio started ringing until all the lines were jammed."
Even people who called in were weeping.

"The phones went crazy," recalled Betty Alvin, a telethon volunteer. As fast as the operators could write a
partner pledge, another call was waiting:

"I want to give $500."

"I'm going to send the insurance refund I got in the
mail today."

"Our church is going to start giving $30 every
month."

"I want to pledge a week's salary."

The calls grew heavier as the telethon went on into the night. Dozens of people said they were awakened out of their sleep and turned on the television.

They pledged.

Cars began arriving at 1318 Spratley Street. People were saying, "I couldn't get through on the phone. Here's my check. We want to be part of CBN."

By 2:30 a.m. a total of $105,000 had been raised. The station signed off the air.

But it wasn't over.

Bill Garthwaite remembers coming over to the station at 6 a.m. Monday to sign the station on the air. "The phones were ringing off the hooks," he recalled with amazement.

That night when WYAH went back on the air, people were still giving. But the station began receiving calls from people who were asking for spiritual help.

People began to arrive at the studio to tell amazing stories of what was happening in their lives.

On Tuesday night, Robertson announced that they needed to increase the size of the studio. He told the viewers that the time was now. Immediately, people began to pledge manpower, building materials and more funds to CBN.

The telethon continued all week.

People all over the area were glued to their TV sets. Local newspapers were receiving calls saying, "This is the most exciting thing that has ever happened in Tidewater."

The past-due bills were all paid.

The budget was totally underwritten.

Robertson's dream began to unfold at a faster pace.

The events of 1966, however, were of deep concern to Robertson. His father, the U.S. senator, had suffered his heartbreaking political defeat at the hands of the Byrd organization. Capital outlays at CBN were straining the operating budget.

When telethon time arrived in November 1966, the budget had grown to $150,000. Plus, the station needed an additional $30,000 down payment on a new transmitter.

Stuart Hamblen flew in from California. He was the gifted songwriter who had become a convert in Billy Graham's 1949 Los Angeles crusade.

Now 12 phone lines were in the studios. They were tied up constantly. In just three days the entire budget was pledged plus the money for the transmitter.

A great percentage of the calls, however, were not "faith promises" of support. They were people who were requesting prayer.

The next day the staff met and it was decided that, considering the great interest of the audience, a nightly show needed to be added.

Since Pat had begun the fund-raiser as the "700 Club" telethon, they decided to call the new show *The 700 Club*. The program made its debut at 10 p.m. on November 28, 1966. It was a team effort with a number of hosts, including Pat Robertson, Jim Bakker and John Gilman.

Every night, the phones would ring constantly. Telephone counselors were trained. All kinds of needs in the community began to be addressed. Referrals were starting to be given to social agencies. Churches were getting involved in following up those with special needs.

The show became the major turning point for CBN.

"No longer did we have to wait from telethon to telethon for finances," recalled a former executive. "When our budget was in need, we shared it with our partners and they responded."

For example, on *The 700 Club* in August 1967 the idea for CBN to go color was talked about. Robertson learned that RCA had two 141-C color cameras for sale for $70,000. They normally sold for twice that amount.

There was only one minor problem. RCA would need a 10 percent down payment within 24 hours to hold the cameras.

Before the show was over, the money was raised.

The program was simultaneously broadcast over WXRI-FM and that night a man in Goldsboro, North

Carolina, 180 miles away, phoned in a pledge and wound up talking personally to Pat.

The man's name was Henry Harrison.

Before the conversation ended, Harrison, a veteran of 20 years in broadcasting, said, "I wonder if there might be something at CBN that I might do?"

Harrison worked closely with Pat for eight years.

"Once, after a *700 Club* program that was exceptionally good, we walked out of the studio feeling extremely proud of ourselves. But as we walked into the men's room, it overflowed. There was water everywhere," Harrison said.

"The janitor was gone, so I grabbed a mop and Pat grabbed a bucket." Henry began to laugh but Pat "didn't think it was so funny."

Said Harrison, "I told him, 'Just when our pride balloon gets so big it would explode, something comes along to deflate it.' "

When Harrison got married in 1970, Robertson performed the ceremony.

"A few days after the wedding, I noticed on the marriage certificate that instead of 1970, Pat had written 1917," Harrison recals. When he told him about it, Pat said, "You've got to be kidding. Let me correct that."

Harrison said, "No way."

He told Pat, "To Susan and me, that's just a further confirmation that God joined us together before either one of us was even born."

The unexpected success of *The 700 Club* gave CBN a much more solid base of operation.

But Robertson did not depend entirely on donations to keep CBN aloft. Said one department head, "As the need arose, Pat would seek other means of financing." Even at the very beginning, he went on the air with Jim Coates' $5,000 loan.

When the time came to build the new studio facility at CBN, he turned to a local bank.

Said Pat, "Six years before we had been turned down for a $5,000 loan because we were not in a 'bankable position.' Now, without hesitation, the Citizens' Trust Company gave the green light for a loan of $225,000 on our new building." Ground was broken June 5, 1967.

Because of construction that fall, the November telethon had to be moved to an auditorium in Norfolk. Dale Evans was a guest. The event was scheduled to last all week but by Tuesday night, the $240,000 budget was raised.

As a business enterprise, CBN was expanding rapidly. The radio station accepted commercials and had a growing sales force in the area.

It was during this time that Channel 27 began "selling spots" on a selective basis.

Revenues at CBN had come a long way. From a $7,000 income for all of 1961, the November 1968 telethon raised $393,000.

Here's how Robertson described CBN's balance sheet to a reporter from the *Norfolk Virginian-Pilot* on May 18, 1969. "We receive about $10,000 a month from radio commercials and about $2,500 a month for TV commercials. Our monthly operating budget is between $50,000 and $60,000."

At the time, CBN's staff had about 40 full-time and 20 part-time employees.

The 1968-69 fiscal year was the first time CBN hit the million-dollar mark — $1,159,000. That included a gift of five radio stations in New York valued at $600,000.

The New York stations were just a part of the national and international involvement CBN was contemplating. The network added a radio station in Bogota, Colombia, South America. Then, it added Channel 46 in Atlanta.

When Robertson had heard about the chance of getting five radio stations in the state of New York, he was told, "They're being offered for $600,000 but I'm sure you can get them for half that amount." The stations, called the Northeast Radio Network, reached Ithaca, Buffalo, Rochester, Albany and Syracuse.

Robertson, remembering his RCA negotiations in the Channel 27 affair, said, "Give us the stations and we will give you a tax-deductible receipt for the market value of $600,000."

The stations were owned by Continental Telephone Company, with headquarters in Bakersfield, California. When Robertson's proposal crossed the desk of the vice president and comptroller, Rucker Arnold, he said, "Oh, yes, I know all about CBN. My brother-in-law, Neil Eskelin, used to work for them. They're a fine organization and I think it's a good deal for our company. I approve it."

Robertson's "network" was taking shape.

A key to the new programming efforts was Scott Ross, a former rock-and-roller who had married a girl named Nedra, who had been featured with the pop group The Ronettes.

Scott sent shock waves through the conservative religious community with his rock-gospel format.

The real statement, however, was that Robertson was willing to withstand criticism in order to reach a new audience with his message. He was not uncomfortable with new formats and concepts.

The demands of an expanding network were costly. The stations in New York had old transmitters that were in need of major repair. The FCC gave the go-ahead for the Atlanta TV station and a total equipment package was needed. Plus, Portsmouth was overdue for a new production center.

When the word got out, bids were coming in from all sides.

But it narrowed down to RCA.

Pat almost choked when he heard the low bid: $3.3 million.

For Robertson, however, that was just the starting point. Before he had finished, Pat had RCA agreeing to an extremely low down payment, a year's moratorium on payments, a long-term payout and very low interest rates. Plus, CBN could control the timing of purchases.

Even with those concessions, Pat was not finished. He got RCA to agree to a $58,000 trade-in on the old transmitter, plus a clause that gave CBN a right to back out of the deal if it could not raise the down payment. The final price came to $2,528,000.

Robertson responded, "Drop the $28,000 and we've got a deal." It was the sixth largest order RCA had ever received from a single customer.

The phenomenal growth of CBN was not always smooth. There were legal skirmishes, tax battles and press criticism.

In 1970, a campaign began to challenge the network's proposed broadcast tower. Critics said it would present a dangerous hazard to pilots approaching the local airport.

But the Federal Aeronautics Administration sided with Robertson and CBN and approved the tower's construction.

The following year, the city of Portsmouth gave Pat a surprise. It presented CBN with a $25,000 tax bill for delinquent property taxes on equipment.

Pat contended that in the eyes of the federal Internal Revenue Service, CBN was a non-profit, tax-exempt organization that did not have to pay the tax.

The city disagreed.

Protesting, he agreed to pay, then scored a public relations coup by "walking the second mile." He presented the city with a check for twice that amount — $50,000.

Said a local merchant, "Robertson made a lot of points on that one."

The audience for *The 700 Club* continued to grow. The "Jim and Tammy" show was now sponsored by Sunbeam Bread.

Then Bakker resigned on November 8, 1972. He went on to build the PTL Television Network. Bakker resigned as president of PTL in March 1987 in what became one of the nation's most widely discussed news stories.

Starting in 1972, CBN began to purchase time for *The 700 Club* on television stations in a growing number of markets. Robertson's role as host was clearly established and CBN's "network" reached coast-to-coast. When a telethon was held, calls not only came in from

Tidewater but from all across America. Additional phone banks were added on a permanent basis to handle thousands of calls coming in day and night. It was CBN's phone number that people felt they could call when they needed comfort and help.

Henry Harrison — today a regular on the PTL network — recalls the time he and Pat flew out to Fresno, California, to do a fund-raiser with CBN partners in the city's civic center.

"The facility was made up of three parts: an auditorium, a sports arena and a large community meeting room. When we drove up to the center, we just could not believe the sign," said Harrison.

The marquee read,

"Van Cliburn
"Wrestling
"Pat Robertson."

Pat looked at the sign and said, "I know Van" — the famous classical piano virtuoso — "is supposed to have strong hands but I believe I could take him at least two falls out of three."

9

Cape Henry Connection

"I remember Pat telling me that one of these days I'd turn on my TV in Atlanta and see him," recalls Buddy Glasgow. "And I'll be derned if that weren't the case. I turned the tube on one day and — there he was!"

Glasgow wasn't alone.

Pat Robertson's face began turning up on American television sets with increasing frequency during the early 1970s. No longer was *The 700 Club* the anchor program for Channel 27 in Portsmouth. It was a nationally syndicated feature of the Christian Broadcasting Network ... which was actually turning into a network.

"Almost overnight, we were in the videotape duplication business," said a CBN broadcast engineer. The live show from Portsmouth had to be recorded, then sent nationwide to be seen on stations where CBN was buying air time.

It was during this period that Robertson established the program as an "issues-oriented" talk show. "Sure, there were guests plugging their books and an emphasis on prayer for the needs of viewers," said a former producer, "but what came through loud and clear was Pat's immense knowledge of national and international issues."

Robertson's audience was growing. No longer was he a "guest host" in rotation with other CBN staffers. When people tuned in, they expected to see Pat — and they did.

As a syndicated show, *The 700 Club* set off a growth cycle at CBN unlike anything Robertson had experienced. Phone calls were coming in by the thousands. The production center was becoming state-of-the-art. And CBN was being presented with a dazzling array of broadcast opportunities.

Robertson was also expanding on other fronts. The National Counseling Center was opened at CBN headquarters in Virginia. And a Canadian office was opened since time was being purchased on stations north of the border.

In the years between 1967 and 1975, CBN's potential audience had grown from 10 million to 110 million. Obviously, the facilities in Portsmouth couldn't contain the growth of CBN. Video productions were scheduled back to back, the National Counseling Center (and 33 local centers around the country) were taking in more than 500,000 calls annually. "Every inch of space at the Spratley Street building was being used to the max," said a video engineer.

Starting in 1975, Robertson began to search for a site where CBN could "stretch and grow." They needed a new headquarters.

Pat thought he had found the ideal spot in Virginia Beach. "It was only five acres but I felt it was perfectly suitable for our plans." There was only one problem. The five acres were part of a much larger tract of land and the owners would not sell only a parcel. It was all or nothing.

To purchase several hundred acres seemed out of the question. CBN's financial position would not allow it.

That summer, in August 1975, Robertson was invited to speak at a convention in Anaheim, California. One day, at noon, he went to a restaurant for lunch. As Pat tells it, when he bowed his head to say grace for the meal, something sparked inside him that unlocked possibilities he had never before imagined. "Don't buy just five acres," an inner voice seemed to be saying. "Buy the entire tract of land and build a headquarters and a school."

Later, Pat discovered the significance of the new location. Just 12 miles to the east, hundreds of years earlier, 104 exhausted settlers and 40 seamen had landed on the shores to found the first English settlement in the New World — Jamestown. In April 1607, they had gathered at a spot they named "Cape Henry" and planted a cross. History records the settlers offered a prayer of thanksgiving and held a brief dedication ceremony, committing the land to God. They declared, "... from these very shores the Gospel shall go forth to not only this New World but the entire world."

Robertson's own personal vision for the Virginia Beach property was all-consuming. When he returned from the West Coast, he was not talking about a new headquarters building, or just a "school." Again, Robertson was seeing things "not as they were but as they were going to be." Now he was talking about an "International Communications Center," and a "major university."

Robertson closed the sale on the property on New Year's Eve, 1975. It was prime acreage, adjoining a major expressway.

But financing the network's aggressive growth was no easy task. It involved advertising sales, telethons, direct mail campaigns, bank notes and more. The activities of the stewardship department in the early 1970s, however, resulted in headlines Robertson did not welcome. In 1975, the federal Securities and Exchange Commission contended Robertson's people were not telling the full story in the presentations. A substantial amount of CBN expansion funds were coming from small investors who were asked to loan money to the network.

As one observer said, "The SEC charged that the fundraising techniques employed amounted to selling unregistered securities and that CBN was not divulging complete financial information to its investors."

Robertson denied impropriety but, to avoid the expense of protracted litigation, signed a "consent agreement" pledging to stop such practices.

"Actually," said a staffer, "it was one of the better things to happen at CBN. It immediately strengthened both internal and external accountability."

It was ironic, however, that between the time the

SEC was charging that CBN finances were in a state of "steady decline" and the announcement of the agreement the network's balance sheet had gone from red to black.

Contributions alone in 1976 reached $20 million.

The 700 Club, called by a critic in Buffalo, "a *Tonight Show* without the lifted eyebrows and the leering jokes," was establishing itself firmly in major cities, one by one.

As Robertson told Michael Connor of the *Wall Street Journal,* "We decided that if the best minds in the business had spent years and years trying to develop a successful format, we'd use that." He added, "We don't have joke writers but we enjoy what we're doing."

In addition to the "stars of the evangelical circuit," such as Charles Colson, Anita Bryant and Galloping Gourmet Graham Kerr, Robertson began to attract more of the world's newsmakers.

For example, the morning after his 1976 election, Robertson ran an exclusive interview with Jimmy Carter. And it was on his show that Israeli Prime Minister Yitzhak Rabin first made public his desire to see a federated Palestine state within Israel.

On January 25, 1977, a tall, dignified gentleman, Ben Kinchlow, joined *The 700 Club* as co-host.

Kinchlow, a Texan and Malcolm X enthusiast on his way to becoming a black revolutionary, had been converted to Christianity. He was invited to be a guest on Robertson's Dallas TV station.

"The next thing I knew," said Ben, "I had a call from Portsmouth." As they ushered him out to the set of *The 700 Club,* the producer said, "Pat's in Israel — you're the host."

Kinchlow developed quickly into a television personality of his own. "He was the perfect sidekick for Pat," said a CBN executive. "Kinchlow has a mind so deep and a wit so quick," said one observer, "that Pat himself is sometimes broken up on the air by Ben's comments."

In 1977, CBN paid nearly $9 million to stations to carry *The 700 Club.* One station alone, WPIX-TV in

New York City, cost CBN approximately $500,000 a year. Robertson's "network" for *The 700 Club* had grown to 36 stations (six VHF and 30 UHF outlets). And CBN's marketing expert, Scott Hessek, was gunning for more.

He told a reporter for *Television/Radio Age* magazine, "We are an alternative to the Sunday ghetto. We're on in most markets five to seven days a week." Hessek added, "The small audiences are getting bigger. In some markets, we have religious shows on UHF channels that are competitive with entertainment programming."

For example, in 1973 Robertson was offered a Dallas TV station as a gift — if he would accept its debts with it. Doubleday, Inc. had tried unsuccessfully to operate KXTX-TV (Channel 39) as a commercial venture.

Under CBN management, KXTX-TV was not only in the black by 1975, it was being hailed as a phenomenal success. *Texas Monthly* magazine called it "the most successful self-supporting Christian television station in the world."

Then something else happened in 1977, on April 29, that forever changed the face of CBN. The "vision" Robertson had in the early 1960s for satellite TV came to reality. CBN officially threw the switch on its own earth satellite station — beaming the CBN signal heavenward to bounce off of communications satellites orbiting Earth.

The industry magazine *Broadcasting* singled out CBN as the leader among all station operators, religious and secular, for the direction it had taken in satellite.

"Robertson wasn't playing follow-the-leader in satellite broadcasting, " said a commercial broadcaster. "He was the leader."

To demonstrate the dramatic potential of satellite, in August 1977 CBN featured live telecasts from five continents culminating in a "feed" from the Mount of Olives in Jerusalem.

Before 1977 had ended, CBN had the distinction of being the largest syndicator of satellite-transmitted programs in the United States.

"The cost of our satellite uplink seemed enormous at

first," said a CBN engineer. "But the money we saved by eliminating tape duplication and distribution made it a great investment."

Something else happened, too. The "live" network resulted in instant feedback which produced even more phone calls at the counseling centers. The January 1978 telethon resulted in over $750,000 in pledges.

Over-the-air broadcasters were slow to install satellite dishes receiving CBN programming. In some cases the network actually bought dishes and presented them to stations.

Cable operators were carving out territories in the late 1970s and CBN was on the cutting edge. By 1978, Robertson had signed up cable systems in over 4,000 communities.

Again, CBN was at the top of the industry and *The 700 Club* was reaching millions of homes "free." In fact, other broadcasters were paying CBN — actually buying time on CBN's "delivery system."

Plus the network was advertiser-supported.

If observers still believed Pat Robertson was a small-time television preacher, they were not paying attention.

By the end of 1978, CBN owned WYAH-TV in Portsmouth, WANX-TV in Atlanta, WXNE-TV in Boston, KTXT-TV in Dallas, plus the Norfolk FM station and the five-station CBN radio network in New York state.

And CBN was syndicating *The 700 Club* to over 130 stations including outlets in Latin America, Africa and Asia. The staff now totaled over 700.

What kind of people were being hired at CBN? Robertson told a reporter from *Broadcasting,* "We like people who see the world through the eyes of love and compassion, whose brains aren't all fogged up with too much booze or too much extracurricular activity."

When asked about the growing news operation, Robertson said that rather than stressing religion, CBN wanted "people who are moral, clean-living individuals." At noon each day, nearly everyone on staff met in the chapel for a 30-minute prayer service.

But the staff wasn't the only thing growing. Plans for the new CBN facility at the Virginia Beach property were dramatic. When Robertson heard what a contractor was asking, he was in a state of shock. "The builder wanted an enormous deposit before he would start building. Two million dollars," said Pat. "They started with the legal restrictions and contracts before we even signed an agreement.

"A friend of mine who has been in real estate development advised me that the minute our building started, the builder would be the enemy. I would be fighting for the next eighteen months. He suggested we get a person with building experience to advise us and represent our interests."

As they discussed it more, "He advised me to form my own company. I told him that we would undertake it if he would be our expert advisor."

Robertson started his own company and it worked out well.

During construction, he said, "We have been able to work at our own pace. If we want to make changes, we know that we are not being taken advantage of."

The projects generated headlines but they were not always positive.

For example, in 1978 the state of Massachusetts sued CBN under a state law requiring charities to disclose their finances. The reorganization of CBN, which created a for-profit division named Continental Broadcasting Network, satisfied the state and the suit was dropped.

Closer to home, the city of Virginia Beach made what Robertson deemed to be an unrealistic claim against CBN in a tax dispute.

Pat didn't hesitate to tackle the issue head-on. In a November 1978 letter to a Virginia Beach tax official, Robertson wrote, "The issue is not taxes but public attacks (for which our only defense is to move or sharply curtail our operations). To quote a popular saying, 'You don't shoot Santa Claus.'"

That same year, *Broadcasting* magazine, in its indepth review of Robertson, said, "A former Democratic congressman from Virginia who knew Dr. Robertson in his youth called him a 'remarkable man' and a 'true Christian.' A Tidewater area newspaper reporter confessed that after almost two years of digging he had been unable to find any improprieties at CBN or among its officials."

The report continued, "A local city editor said Dr. Robertson was a 'genius.' A news director of a local television station said he was 'not even sure there was a whistle to be blown' at CBN. Even one disgruntled former employee, who punctuated his comments with references to 'Saint Patrick,' concluded after several years with CBN that Dr. Robertson and the majority of his associates were, indeed, sincerely religious persons."

The questions regarding Robertson were more often concerned with size than with substance. "The fact that Pat had a national audience of millions creates no small amount of jealousy," said one CBN aide.

Robertson, speaking on the issue, told a reporter, "There are always little people who will want to bring people down. The issue is not success or size but service." Pat asked, "How many people do you want to serve? If you want to serve a hundred, your budget will be modest. If you want to serve 700 million like we do, then your budget will be larger." And he added, "The per capita expenditure won't be any more but the total expense of reaching these people will be."

Pat has also been charged with "draining the local church" because people send their gifts to a long-distance television ministry. When a religious publication, *Your Church,* posed the question in 1979, Robertson said, "We've just completed a survey among our contributors by an independent research organization. Results affirm that participation in a national broadcasting ministry such as CBN stimulates people to increase their activity in the local church."

"Seventy percent of them actually give more money to their local church after they start contributing to CBN," responds Robertson. "They are better church members and they work harder in their local church."

Regardless of the evidence, or even Robertson's logic, critics continued to pound away at the concept of large-scale media evangelism.

But Robertson is firmly convinced that his methods and his message have been a great boon to America's faith and to churches in every city in the nation.

Says Pat, "We have a chance to heighten their faith beyond anything that they would find in the average church." He was speaking about the fact that the average church meets 60 minutes each Sunday and hears a 20-minute sermon. Robertson reaches them for 90 minutes daily.

"We are like an advance party. We're reaching out where people are — in their homes. And we can be the first contact they have with religion." Robertson feels *The 700 Club* is like an advertisement, a "teaser" which attracts people to come to the main performance.

William Martin, author of a book on media ministry, said of Robertson's approach, "Though ... evangelism strikes many — Christians and non-Christians alike — as intellectually inappropriate for a post-Enlightenment world, it is nevertheless espoused by millions of Americans, from Baptists to Roman Catholics. *The 700 Club* version of it is sufficiently simple and broad enough to be acceptable to all but the most sectarian of these."

What has surprised many observers has been the deep support of Catholics for Robertson's projects.

"When Robertson reads from the Scriptures he exudes a child-like wonder that almost makes you forget that he has a law degree from Yale and was Phi Beta Kappa from Washington and Lee University. There is an aura of simplicity and sincerity about the man so that when he exhorts viewers to read the Bible when they stop at a traffic light, no one in the live audience snickers," wrote David Strack in *Richmond* magazine in December 1979.

By the fall of 1979, two enormous Williamsburg-style brick buildings were completed at the Virginia Beach property. One is an administrative and classroom building for the university. The second, CBN Center, is headquarters for the network and studios for programs, including *The 700 Club.*

The production center was almost more than the staff in Portsmouth could imagine. And the first time I saw it, I pinched myself and asked, "Is this really CBN?"

With a touch of a button, a computer-based system allows dozens of pieces of scenery to be moved at one time. And the lighting system not only heats the studios in winter but also provides warmth for the rest of the sprawling headquarters building.

One guest described it as "the ultimate television facility." From the makeup room to the editing suites, CBN had not only caught up with the broadcast industry but was now leading it. Outside, the landscaping was something out of a design book.

Here's how writer Dick Dabney lavishly described it in *Harper's* magazine.

He saw "long hedges of Japanese holly and panels of green lawn adjacent to the vivid reds of the brick sidewalks and the brick arches to the side of the buildings accented by full-grown native American holly and Southern magnolia — while along the walkways there were the Natchez White crepe myrtles set in pleasant beds of ivy and periwinkle."

And if that weren't enough, he continued, "Even the trees around the place were, in the words of Keats, 'dear as the temple's self,' and interspersed with the native pines were dogwood, forsythia, magnolia, azaleas, hemlock, juniper, October Glory maple, boxwood ... and viburnum, to say nothing of petunias, geraniums and chrysanthemums."

Classan Avenue was nothing like this.

The dedication of the new headquarters on October 6, 1979, attracted a "Who's Who" of the evangelical world. Billy Graham gave the keynote address. Also present were Rex Humbard and Bill Bright of Campus Crusade.

But it was the growth of CBN's "telephone hotline" connected to dozens of counseling centers that became a key to Robertson's success. "There are millions of people who desperately want somebody to answer their questions," said Pat.

"If a hotline connected to a church were available, churches would be overrun with people. It would be helpful if people could talk to a person they trusted, who wouldn't tell their secrets and who would listen to their problems and give them psychological and spiritual counseling."

Said Robertson, "They are afraid to go to church because they don't know the Sunday morning ritual and they are afraid to ask questions in public for fear of being dumb. That's why a telephone hotline is so important."

As the calls kept pouring in, Robertson juggled his daily schedule as a television host, father, business executive, author and university chancellor. "When I get to the office, I take off my ministry cap and put on my business cap," he told *TV Guide*'s Paul Hemphill.

The 1970s were coming to a close but Robertson was just beginning to flex his media muscle. "The satellite," he said, "is our slingshot against the three Goliaths." He was referring to ABC, NBC and CBS. "The resources and power of the networks are unbelievable. They can spend $600 million a year or more on programming alone — pilots, canceled programs, talent — and we can't come anywhere near that. We're small but we can turn faster and adjust just like small ships."

Robertson's firmly held belief that the future was with family programming and meeting human need was like a magnet pulling him forward. He believed CBN was destined to become more than a network. Much more.

"When a child becomes a man, he becomes concerned with how effective he is, whether or not what he is doing is useful, whether the things he is doing are amounting to anything," said Robertson.

As *Broadcasting* magazine observed, "Pat Robertson is a committed man who believes CBN can and will equal and perhaps surpass the powers of American and world television. Said Robertson, 'We're not blue-sky speculators; we're going to have to take it one bite at a time.' "

10

Star Trek

"He's going to be a little late," said Pat Robertson's appointment secretary. I was waiting for him in Springfield, Missouri, where I was living at the time.

It was March 1981. Pat was to address a Communications Award Banquet at Evangel College that night.

The secretary had phoned to tell me Pat had to be in San Diego that morning, Dallas for an afternoon meeting and would be flying into Springfield at about 5 p.m.

The airport security guard told me I could drive my car to where his little jet would park, since we were running short of time.

On the tarmac, I watched the small, sleek jet land. Out hopped an energetic Robertson. He walked over to my car, marvelling at it. "Neil, what are you doing driving a Cadillac Coupe deVille?" he exclaimed.

"Well," I responded, grinning, "what are you doing flying around in a private jet?"

We had both come a long way. Robertson's lifestyle had dramatically changed but so had his responsibilities. To him, being allowed the use of an executive jet made it possible to accomplish in one day what would normally take three. And to him that was wise use of time.

At the banquet, Pat was pushing for excellence. "There is a desperate need for committed, trained leaders in every area of public life. And it takes much more than merely being a Christian," he said. "It takes a commitment to excellence and a passion for quality. There really is no limit to what can be accomplished."

Robertson, in the 1980s, had seen enough dreams come true to last a lifetime but he was not through. His plans for CBN were lofty.

Pat's decision to program his stations and the satellite network with predominantly secular programming, however wholesome, set off a storm of controversy within religious broadcasting circles.

When there was only one religious television station in 1961, no one paid much attention to the schedule, since the impact was so small. But now there were dozens of "Christian" television stations on the air and station managers were taking sides as to how they should be operated.

Even the annual convention of the National Religious Broadcasters, which attracts thousands to its Washington, D.C., event, got involved. In the early 1980s they scheduled seminars on the "secular vs. religious" format question.

Jerry Rose, a former CBN operations manager and now president of Chicago's Christian television voice, Channel 38, took the side of the "purist."

Said Rose, "Our mission is to reach our cities with a message. Why should we dilute our purpose by filling our schedule with Hollywood reruns?"

CBN's David Clark retorted, "We have the same mission. But isn't it logical to attract a large audience first and then present your message?"

With few exceptions, most so-called "Christian" television stations followed CBN's lead.

Economic survival was the reason most religious broadcasters turned to blocks of westerns, comedies and quiz shows.

Robertson's stations in Norfolk, Atlanta, Boston and Dallas were promoting *The Lucy Show* and *Star Trek*.

On the satellite-to-cable front the same argument prevailed. CBN, when first promoted in the late 1970s, was the Christian alternative cable operators added to help sign up subscribers.

Slowly, however, CBN began to reflect its new slogan, "The Family Entertainer." And, with the exception of *The 700 Club* and a few weekend religious blocks, Robertson's network was clearly in the ratings war.

"It was Pat's Dallas station that opened his eyes to the potential of reaching large audiences," said a former CBN programmer.

"All across the country, cartoons have kept the independent stations alive," said CBN's Roger Baerwolf, then general manager of the Dallas station. He told a reporter for *Texas Monthly* that family-oriented reruns were not only economically necessary but were what attracted people to the "electronic church."

Said Baerwolf, "When we ran only Christian shows, we were doing a pretty good job of edifying the church," but the station was not reaching its objective. "We had an audience (in Dallas) of about thirty thousand households a week. Now that we use the family-oriented programs, we reach about six hundred thousand households per week and we get a ten percent share of the audience in the early fringe period, from 4 to 7 p.m."

The station also found its niche in the marketplace with aggressive live sports coverage. But it was a local kids show, *Good Time Gang,* that demonstrated the influence of media on young people.

The *Gang,* which sponsored rallies, parties and outings for children in the Metroplex, had, at one time, over 120,000 card-carrying members. It was so big that it was almost impossible to have an event of any kind since no facility in the area could contain the crowds.

My return visits to be a guest on *The 700 Club* in the early '80s were a study in contrasts. They were anniversary shows and we were to talk about the pioneering days in Portsmouth but what was most noticeable was the revolution in format Robertson's program had achieved.

Producer Michael Little handed me a breakdown of the show that contained dozens of tightly formatted segments. Some units were as short as 20 seconds. The "magazine" format was eons away from the Robertson I remember who talked past the scheduled signoff on Channel 27.

What was also surprising was the fact that the guest

list did not include non-stop "born-again" believers. If someone were an authority on heart disease, he was scheduled for his information, not inspiration — Pat could handle that part.

And that was his goal for the viewing audience, too. "Robertson decided not just to seek men and women who agree with the Bible," said William Barry Furlong in *The Saturday Evening Post*. "He decided to reach out also to those other men and women who know nothing about the Bible."

Said Furlong, "He knew he could not preach the gospel alone; most of the people simply wouldn't listen. What he had to do was offer them a special bait, to lure them with something they already knew they needed: the information to make life richer."

It was the summer of 1980 when Pat began offering a healthy dose of secular information on *The 700 Club*.

On a typical day, the format for *The 700 Club* contains three distinct 30-minute segments. As one observer put it, "The first half-hour is a secular smorgasbord, the next is half-and-half, the final 30 minutes is no-holds-barred, spiritual inspiration."

And how does the secular society receive Robertson? Said *Harper's* magazine writer Dick Dabney, "He did not come on like a preacher at all; he was no thundering sermoneer nor twittering-birds smirker but a reasonable and educated man, with a unified point of view that was especially intriguing to intellectuals." He added, "Although, as for that, his appeal was broad and he had the Grand Old Opry crowd as well."

The new format fit Robertson like a tailor-made suit. It made him look good. Those long years in academia had not been wasted. Not one minute. Pat was as comfortable discussing stock market cycles as he was with the philosophies of Socrates and Plato.

Then there was politics.

Robertson had never been shy when it came to issues but in 1980 he pulled out all the stops to promote a national gathering in the nation's capital. It was called "Washington for Jesus."

The April 29 event which attracted a massive turnout estimated at 500,000 people to Capitol Hill featured Pat Robertson as the keynote speaker. That event demonstrated to both the press and official Washington that the evangelicals were coming out of their isolation. They were a formidable force that must be reckoned with.

As one Washington writer put it, "... in the crowd itself, one got jolted by excitement that could not be transmitted by any television camera."

Looking back on the event, Robertson has called it "one of the greatest moments in the history of America." There are many who attribute the election of Ronald Reagan to the message that was carried from Washington that day. Said Robertson, "We've had a revolution in this country since that Washington rally."

Clearly, the signal was given that the decade of the '80s would be a "turning point" in America. A sleeping giant was emerging that would have a decided impact on the nation's future. Robertson was being hailed as spokesman for that giant. Loyal viewers of *The 700 Club* were noting another trend. There was a growing emphasis on news coverage. Late-breaking stories became an instant addition to the format. CBN's Washington bureau was establishing itself as a viable news source.

On the international scene, Robertson's influence was being felt. CBN had expanded its activities to include projects in over 70 nations. The "Star of Hope" TV station in South Lebanon, opened in 1982, was a highly visible example of CBN's world presence.

The foreign impact, however, was not all visual. Massive food relief efforts were saving thousands of lives. In 1982, Robertson was awarded the annual Humanitarian Award from Food for the Hungry. It was presented by the organization's president, Larry Ward, for Pat's having shown compassion for needy people outside the United States.

The impact has been felt inside the United States, too.

On the West Coast, at his home in Escondido, California, Harald Bredesen had just spent three hours answering a volley of questions about Christianity from a local philosophy discussion group. In the group was Danuta Soderman, co-host of *Sun-Up San Diego,* a local morning TV talk show.

Danuta, who was into everything from tarot cards to transcendental meditation, made a commitment to Christianity that night at Bredesen's home. Almost immediately, her daily talk show duties seemed meaningless. "I was taking up time and space, entertaining people with vacuous, innocuous details that didn't mean anything to anybody," said Danuta.

Bredesen encouraged her to send *The 700 Club* an audition tape. Nine months later she heard a response. Someone had found her package unopened in a desk. She was invited for an audition and two weeks later, on March 13, 1983, she made her debut as co-host with Kinchlow and Robertson.

As the format of *The 700 Club* continued to be refined, the platform allowed Robertson to establish himself as an authority on a wide variety of topics. One feature in particular became enormously popular. It was a spot that featured questions from the audience on whatever topic they chose. "It almost became a 'Can you stump Pat?' spot on the show," said a CBN executive.

Questions ranged from infidelity to international monetary reforms. Robertson was never at a loss for words. In fact, the feature resulted in a book that appeared on bestseller charts, *Answers to 200 of Life's Most Probing Questions.*

Financially, CBN's annual income was continuing to grow but resources were stretched to the limits. The economics of Robertson's empire were strengthened, however, by the decreasing reliance on donor dollars for survival. The "bottom line" of CBN-owned-and-operated broadcast stations made it possible to tap financial institutions for long-term funds. Advertising sales on the satellite network were increasing. The operations budget for the university was becoming manageable on a current basis. The donor base widened, too. In the 1960s and 1970s, the emphasis was on the $10 per month partner.

By 1982, over 300,000 people were donating $15 a month for the projects of CBN. More than 150,000 others were giving on an annual basis. Yearly income from all sources had passed $100 million a year.

Who were the donors? One CBN survey showed that about 16 percent were Baptists, with significant percentages of Methodists, Roman Catholics and members of the Assemblies of God, plus healthy support from non-denominational Christians.

How does Robertson appeal to such a diverse audience? "We don't insult their beliefs and we don't take partisan issues that would inflame, say, Protestant vs. Catholic," he says.

Ben Kinchlow's presence as co-host for over a decade has given Robertson a solid base of support among the black community.

The sophistication of satellite technology made another mode of fund-raising possible. In the early 1980s, simultaneous events in hotels and banquet halls across the nation linked CBN partners together for a single rally. As noted by Bill McKay in his book, *Vital Signs,* "Robertson invited 165,000 supporters to a special event. Dispersed across 217 cities in the United States and seven more in Canada, CBN collected $6.5 million that evening against program costs of $950,000."

Robertson's personal finances, like those of all heads of television empires, are constantly the subject of media scrutiny. The days of Pat's $100 weekly stipend are gone but CBN has regularly reported his salary. In 1986 that income from CBN was $60,335. According to Robertson aides, he donates a substantial portion of his salary back to the network. Additional income is provided from book royalties.

A controversy also surrounded the building of the Robertsons' new home.

What the press wanted to know was, "Where is the money coming from to build it?" The answer, according to CBN officials, was rather simple. Pat was paying for the residence with book royalties, then donating the home back to the university.

The privacy of the Robertsons is a matter of continuing concern. "Anyone with as much television exposure as Pat receives all kinds of physical threats," said an aide. "then there are well-meaning people who would dominate his entire day if we didn't have security to keep him on schedule."

Here's how one observer, James Wooten, in *Southern Magazine,* described his security: "Using a sophisticated radio-communications system, they're in constant contact with a central command post in the bowels of the nearby headquarters building of CBN. In fact, Robertson is almost as well protected from the outside world as any president, surrounded ... by bodyguards who wear little buttons in their lapels *a la* the Secret Service's presidential detail."

Robertson's schedule is precise. "He accomplishes more in one day than most men do in one week," said an employee. "He's not afraid to make decisions, however painful."

Not all of Robertson's announced plans have come to pass. Even some that have were canceled when it became obvious there was no public support, or economics dictated the decision.

Another Life, described as a "Christian soap opera," is a good example. In the late 1970s, CBN executives were touting the concept with unbridled enthusiasm. Said Tucker Yates, a long-time Robertson associate, the soap opera would give people answers to the problems the characters face.

When the daily 30-minute show hit the CBN satellite, there was a rush of excitement that surrounded the project — especially from dozens of independent religious television stations that secured rights to air it.

"But that's not what we wanted," said a CBN programmer. "We wanted to be taken seriously by the secular broadcasters and advertisers." Technically and professionally, the effort was outstanding. In fact, many of the leading roles on *Another Life* were played by actors who came to CBN from New York soap operas because they so believed in the new concept.

"The numbers just weren't there," said an audience research analyst. "Advertisers buy viewers; they're not concerned with underwriting production costs."

Finally, Robertson made the decision to halt production. It was not easy. But economically he had no choice.

He has also been as realistic about CBN's news operation. Robertson has been committed to news coverage since George Lauderdale read the headlines on October 1, 1961. At times, he has launched major news thrusts on the network.

In the 1970s, Robertson tried an early morning satellite news and information effort, *U.S.A.M.* Bob Slosser, formerly with *The New York Times,* came to CBN, in part, to direct Pat's news operation. He is now president of CBNU. At the time, Pat said, "We expect our news will cover all the major stories shown on CBS, NBC and ABC. However, we feel that national network news has reflected a bias centered in the Washington-New York axis and we do not intend to follow the lead of two or three national news media giants in deciding what the stories are."

U.S.A.M. was disbanded but the news operation had been firmly established, both through network news breaks and *The 700 Club* updates. *CBN News Tonight,* at 10 p.m. Eastern time on the satellite network premiered January 27, 1986, the day before the space shuttle *Challenger* exploded. The nightly program was headquartered in Washington and was supplemented by bureaus worldwide. It was planned, according to managing editor Don Clark, "to answer the question which is foremost in the American mind: 'What does it mean to me?' "

Robertson cancelled the show two months later because of low advertising revenues. Again, Pat is not shy when it comes to launching new efforts, nor bashful when it comes to cutting his losses. Overall, however, there were more "ups" than "downs." Between September of 1982 and September of 1985, CBN satellite network had doubled — from 14,994,000 homes to 29,714,000 homes. Robertson's "delivery system" was clearly a dominant force in the cable television industry.

It was the Walker spy story, in late summer, 1985, that turned heads toward CBN. Laura Walker Snyder, daughter of accused Soviet spy John Walker, revealed to *The 700 Club* viewers the startling story that her father tried to lure her and other members of the family into the espionage network. Robertson's interview was the first time the nation heard the story of what was becoming "America's most damaging spy case."

She chose CBN to break the story because she had been helped by the counseling ministry of *The 700 Club*. As it was reported, "She knew for years that her father was selling secrets to the Russians, she said, adding that because her estranged husband possessed the same knowledge, he was able to keep her from seeing their five-year-old son, whom he had."

As she told Robertson, her estranged husband had taken the boy after they separated and threatened to tell authorities of her father's alleged involvement with the Soviets if she tried to get the child back. CBN viewers watched as she told that it was the "mounting pressure" of not being with her son, plus counseling she received through *The 700 Club,* that eventually led her to convince her mother to tell the FBI of her father's activities.

Here's what happened, according to a CBN public relations release: "The exclusive CBN interviews spanning two days' programs were picked up on the front pages of every newspaper in the nation as well as by wire services and radio and television stations, most of them crediting CBN for its news break."

"CBS, NBC and ABC may be the big guys on the block," *The Washington Post* stated the day after the first interview was aired, "but from the beginning CBN has owned the story of Laura Walker Snyder ..."

The *Post* told readers CBN had "scooped the world" with its story of the Walker family. But that was not the only "scoop" CBN was sharing. A short time later, CBN's correspondent in Lebanon was the first to announce the names of two hijackers of TWA Flight 847, one of the most dramatic hostage-holding incidents. Plus viewers were first told of the activities of the terrorist group that took over the plane. Robertson made news again, interviewing the brother of Robert Stethem, the U.S. sailor who was murdered by the hijackers.

Besides the headlines being made by the network, Robertson's announcement regarding CBN University made headlines, too. On November 1, 1985, the Board of Regents of Oral Roberts University in Tulsa, Oklahoma, gave its law school to CBN University effective at the close of its 1985-86 academic year. On June 1, 1986, the law school was moved to Virginia Beach and the first class was admitted three months later.

Robertson continues to honor the original founder, O.W. Coburn, whose major financial gift allowed Roberts to start the law school in 1976. The original "statement of vision" is printed in the CBNU catalog. Its objective will be to prepare "well-qualified professionals who will provide leadership as attorneys, judges, politicians and businessmen dedicated to wisdom and truth."

Over 100 students enrolled as the law school opened at CBNU in September 1986. Robertson was elated. The accrediting question presents a major hurdle for Pat but it is one he feels he can win. The facts, according to CBNU, are that, "In August 1981, the American Bar Association granted the O.W. Coburn School of Law of Oral Roberts University provisional accreditation.

"In an effort to retain the provisional accreditation status, officials at ORU filed a petition with the ABA requesting it to acquiesce in the transfer of the law school. In August 1986, the ABA Council of the Section of Legal Education denied the petition for acquiesence. Thus the ABA provisional approval has not transferred to the law school at its new location at CBN University."

Of course, Robertson plans to take every step to secure accreditation and he believes it will happen. But they caution incoming students that "the law school makes no representation to any applicant that it will be approved by the American Bar Association prior to graduation of any matriculating student."

CBN University has also applied both to the Commonwealth of Virginia Council of Higher Education and the Southern Association of Colleges for accreditation toward the doctorate degree. A stamp of approval at this level will make it possible for CBNU to confer the same degree Robertson received at Yale, Juris Doctor.

By 1987, Robertson had a vast "conglomerate" approaching a quarter-billion-dollar annual budget and more than 3,000 employees. Oh, how far it had come:

• A major commercial broadcasting network.

• Counseling centers across the nation tied to *The 700 Club*.

• A graduate university with six schools.

• A multi-million dollar campus and headquarters.

• An international presence in over 70 nations.

• A national literacy program, Heads Up.

• Operation Blessing, helping over 8 million annually with food and clothing.

And there was something else. Robertson was being asked to run for the highest office in the land — president of the United States of America. Back in Lexington, the home folks aren't really surprised. They've come to expect the exceptional from Robertson.

"He hasn't been spoiled by all the notoriety," Matt Paxton told me. He's the editor of the local paper, the *Lexington News and Gazette*. "We were fraternity brothers and he was in our wedding. But he really hasn't changed that much."

Yes, Dr. Marion Gordon Robertson may have hit the big time.

But to many, he's just plain Pat.

11

The Hurricane

Pat Robertson's image as a media executive, academician and commentator on world events has been largely overlooked by those who prefer to paint him as a "televangelist," "faith healer" or "fundamentalist."

The fact that he believes in prayer, whether it be for a headache or a hurricane, has often become the focus of attention, regardless of what topic he might be addressing. The "copycat" nature of journalists has produced a stream of articles on Robertson that have a predictable format. Yes, they talk about his brilliant upbringing but quickly zero in on Pat's faith — complete with an example designed to shock the reader.

"Most people in the secular press don't have the slightest idea of the difference between an evangelical and a fundamentalist," said a Dallas minister who is a Robertson supporter. "They lump them all together as part of the 'new right.' "

Robertson is certainly fundamental in his faith but he should not be called a "fundamentalist." That term is reserved for those individuals who hold to a rather strict doctrine of literal biblical interpretation. In fact, their view is so well defined that "fellowship" with those of other persuasions is discouraged. Jerry Falwell comes from that background.

Robertson is a Southern Baptist. Falwell is a member of the Baptist Bible Fellowship, which is about five paces to the conservative right of the church embraced by Pat. But Robertson has another tag — "evangelical." That term covers a wide variety of Christian denominations whose hallmark is aggressive evangelism with an emphasis on personal conversion. But the evangelicals demonstrate a more moderate attitude toward doctrinal differences than do the fundamentalists.

They form a powerful group, representing millions of church members of more than 70 denominations, called the National Association of Evangelicals. (Southern Baptists are also called evangelicals but stick to themselves and are not members of the NAE).

Pat is also a "charismatic," which means he embraces biblical teachings including faith healing and speaking in tongues — as do over 20 million Americans who cut across every denomination, including Roman Catholics.

While Southern Baptists do not openly endorse "charismatics," they have not shunned Robertson. In fact, Adrian Rogers, president of the Southern Baptist Convention, was the featured speaker at CBN's 25th anniversary.

Where does that leave Robertson? As one observer put it, "He's supported by millions of Baptists and evangelicals, millions of charismatics, millions of Christians in the old-line protestant churches and millions of conservatives." Even Falwell (who demonstrates more tolerance than most of his hard-line followers) was a recent guest on *The 700 Club*.

The 1976 presidential campaign of Jimmy Carter was an education for America on the born-again experience. (In fact, it took several years before the *Washington Post* would print the term without putting it in quotes).

Robertson was a vocal supporter of Carter's nomination and election, as were the vast majority of evangelicals and fundamentalists. But as his presidency wore on, a rising tide of criticism from fellow Christians was being felt in the Oval Office. Pat was one of the critics.

In *Pat Robertson's Perspective,* a monthly CBN publication during the late '70s and early '80s, he described Jimmy Carter as "honest and decent but unsuited for his task."

The number-one criticism by Christians, however,

was not Carter's religious commitment. That, they admired. But they could not understand why his White House team played by a different set of rules.

Robertson recently told a reporter for *Southern Partisan,* "I had lunch two days ago with a former deputy assistant secretary of state who has a degree in psychiatry and who is also a Christian. He said that in his service under Jimmy Carter — which included some crisis negotiation in Iran — it was his feeling that Mr. Carter used his religion to cover up indecision."

ABC network newsman James Wooten said recently, "Having spent so much time with Carter, both as a reporter assigned to his campaign and later as a White House correspondent, I find the comparison between him and Robertson personally unavoidable. Carter, it seems to me, was essentially a religious man who committed himself to politics; Robertson strikes me as a secular man who went into religion. Each brought with him the accoutrements of his original bent. For Carter, that meant a presidency that conveyed the continuing hopelessness of a sinful world and the dour Christian duty of dealing with it as it was, without much promise of a better day."

Adds Wooten, "Not that Carter was a joyless fellow. He wasn't — but his theology was an enlightened, existential fundamentalism that did not lend itself to the country's compulsion to sublimate the bad news. Robertson, in contrast, brings to his religion — and now, in turn, to his politics — the bullish attitudes of a hard-charging businessman, the faith of a Christian entrepreneur who just *knows* that if he gets right and stays right with the Lord, his immediate temporal status will improve."

In 1976, evangelicals, who were just beginning to get involved in national politics, voted for Carter in large numbers. But in the 1980 election, evangelicals cast their ballots for Ronald Reagan over Carter by 56 to 34 percent. (In 1984, nearly 80 percent of born-again Christians voted for Reagan).

On more than one occasion, Robertson has publicly stated that the Washington For Jesus Rally, in April 1980, was a turning point in American politics.

Toward the end of Carter's reign, evangelicals were flexing their political muscle through a number of grassroots organizations. Supreme Court decisions such as *Roe vs. Wade,* on the abortion issue, spurred their involvement.

In May of 1979, Falwell and a group of politicians and preachers of the New Right held a meeting that resulted in the founding of the Moral Majority. Its platform was to "restrict abortion, promote school prayer, control pornography and advance family values." Robertson backed the concept but shied away from a major leadership position.

During the election year of 1980, another group, "The Roundtable," became politically active. The Washington-based Christian organization was led by a "Council of 56" which included Robertson, Falwell and a host of conservative notables. The purpose was to activate evangelicals in the political process, whether Democrat or Republican. The focus was on issues, not candidates.

On the campaign trail, Reagan addressed a Roundtable rally in Dallas, in August 1980. Robertson was on the platform.

The event made headlines when Reagan said, "I know that you can't endorse me but I want you to know that I endorse you."

One month later, Robertson made the surprise announcement that he was resigning from The Roundtable. Pat cited "confusion in the public mind as to my role in political matters" as the major reason for his resignation. He said CBN should focus on the "spiritual" mission instead of politics at that time.

Under a headline that read, "Pat Robertson Backs Away From Politics," his hometown newspaper gave his statement that "I have always been supportive of the Christians' rights to be citizens. Christians have a responsibility to be good citizens: to be informed on issues — to vote." But he said, "We are now faced with the desperate need for a spiritual-moral revival in America. I have nothing against how other ministers see their roles: each must do as he believes best." Then Robertson noted that he would emphasize evangelism rather than political involvement during the next three years.

In a letter to Roundtable president Edward McAteer, Robertson said, "As you know, the press totally misread efforts like Washington For Jesus as being fronts for the 'right.' This was not true and yet nothing we said would convince them. One of the reasons they weren't convinced was my involvement in The Roundtable."

Robertson's resignation sparked a great deal of speculation. Was he breaking from a close association with Falwell? Was he planning a permanent exit from politics? Or did he have a personal agenda that he was not ready to discuss?

The involvement of evangelicals in politics is a topic on which Robertson has more than a casual understanding. In an interview with Wes Michaelson for *Sojourners* magazine in 1979, Pat said, "With the turn of the century the evangelicals retreated from any social consciousness, from the concept of freeing the slaves and helping the oppressed and getting involved in social issues. They withdrew to a fortress and pulled up the gates after them ... the focus of the whole evangelical movement was on the hereafter. We said let's give up on government ... "

The result, said Robertson, was that "by the 1920s the movement of the evangelical people had lost its influence in almost every aspect of society. Well, it's my feeling that the vacuum was filled by people who shared an entirely different worldview than had previously been accepted as the consensus one hundred years prior to that."

That consensus, believes Robertson, is up for grabs. He said, "We represent the vast majority of the people. If you put the Catholics and the evangelicals together, it's a clear majority. It's the silent majority. We don't have a consensus now; that's one of our problems. We ought to fill that gap to formulate a national consensus."

While the idea of a coalition of evangelicals and Catholics seems out of the question to many, Robertson sees it as more than a possibility. As he said in 1980,

"The Holy Spirit is bringing about a true ecumenicity which springs from love and a common faith. There is a fellowship developing between Protestants and Catholics that is absolutely mind-boggling. I don't think we could have dared to believe 10 to 15 years ago that attitudes would change so much."

Robertson believes that, regardless of their church background, committed Christians are getting tired of having to support a Washington establishment that is basically secular.

In the August 1981 issue of his *Perspective,* Pat made the point clear. "To evangelicals," he wrote, "the breakdown of public morality and massive court-ordered restrictions on religious freedoms is the agenda. To them abortion is murder; homosexuality and adultery are grievous sins; and restrictions on prayer and Bible reading are an affront against God. Evangelicals tend to be conservative but sooner or later they will tire of giving support to secular politicians who promise great things, then forget their promises to their evangelical constituents."

Even as the evangelicals began their political and social awakening, they were often ignored by the press — as were their video spokesmen.

"In retrospect," wrote Richard Brookshire recently in the *National Review,* "it is remarkable in that total obscurity, as far as the mainstream culture was concerned, Robertson and his fellow television evangelists labored and grew. Since their religion had nothing to do with German philosophy or atheism, not even religion editors noticed them. The world of the evangelicals was like Atlantis — a sunken continent of behavior and belief."

But once the movement became inescapable, the press, in Robertson's view, did their best to discredit it.

Pat, asked about it recently, said, "Oh, there's no question about it. They know very well if they can identify somebody as a 'right wing fundamentalist,' they have effectively neutralized his intelligence and what he says.

"A case in point," said Robertson, "*Newsweek* in its capsule pages at the beginning of the magazine described Francis Schaffer as a 'fundamentalist propagandist,' or words to that effect. Francis Schaffer was a profound philosopher. He was a scholar. But the minute they identified him as a 'fundamentalist,' they had automatically trivialized him and rendered him impotent. They do it deliberately — there's no question about it. If they had said 'moderate thinker' or 'profound intellectual,' they would have given him status. Instead, by calling him 'a fundamentalist,' they took that away from him."

Robertson himself is often the target of the same type of treatment.

Typical is the caricature of Pat drawn by Vint Lawrence in the September 29, 1986, issue of *The New Republic*. He is depicted as a god-like presence with piercing eyes. His hair — almost on fire — was swept up into a halo. If the idea was to make Pat look frightening, he succeeded.

Among other things, Robertson believes the press is guilty of presenting the movement as a danger to society. Says Pat, "People are portraying evangelicals as wanting to impose their values. All we want is government not to impose socialism on us."

The realities of American politics, however, require social and ideological movements to eventually align themselves with a political party. That certainly happened with the evangelicals.

When recently asked about it by *Christianity Today,* Frank Fahrenkopf, chairman of the Republican National Committee, said, "Since the days of Franklin Roosevelt, self-identification of American voters has been static. About 50 percent of the voters have called themselves Democrats, 25 percent Republicans and 25 percent independents or nonpartisan. Many in all three categories were evangelical Christians and particularly in the South most of them were Democrats.

"Thanks largely to the leadership of President Reagan," says Fahrenkoph, "the breakdown of the American electorate has changed. Today it is 40 percent Democrat, 40 percent Republican and about 20 percent independent. A large portion of the people who moved from a Democratic or independent affiliation are evangelicals. They felt the Republican party has best represented what they wanted for their families, communities and country."

In recent elections, evangelicals have shown surprising strength. Says political observer John B. Judis, "In North Carolina, South Carolina, Tennessee, Kentucky, Illinois, Indiana, Texas, New Mexico, Arizona, Colorado, California, Oregon and Alaska, evangelicals have mounted credible campaigns for major offices." And, says Judis, "They have succeeded in rewriting party platforms to endorse not just school prayer and a ban on pornography and abortion (under all circumstances) but also even more controversial stands favoring creationism and the quarantine of AIDS victims and decrying the 'separation' between church and state."

While the media has been painting the politically active evangelicals as the "New Right," Robertson has another view: "I like to think of us as the new center rather than the right."

The shift Robertson is talking about is attributed by many to be the direct result of the influence of television evangelists. Dr. Jeffrey Hadden, the University of Virginia sociology professor who is a leading expert on the phenomenon, says the conservative religious audience is "potentially as large a base of group support as any interest group in America."

Hadden believes that there is no single element in America large enough to win a national election but believes the religious audience is enormous when both their size and intensity are combined. Plus, he has found a strong correlation between the television media ministries and the political right. In analyzing more than 80 syndicated religious television shows, Hadden says, "All but a tiny handful are politically conservative."

In a recent study by the Gallup organization and the University of Pennsylvania's Annenburg School of Communication, it was found that it is not the size of the audience but the activism that makes it potentially so effective at the polls.

"Heavy viewers of religious programs are more likely than non-viewers to describe themselves as conservatives, oppose a nuclear freeze, favor tougher laws against pornography and report voting in the last general election," the study reported.

The researchers added, "The coherent mobilizing power of religious television, rather than its reach or scope, represents its political clout."

Robertson's critics, particularly the People for the American Way organization, seem frightened enough by his media power to make him a special target. Says PAW president Anthony Podesta, "Jerry Falwell was investing in balloons and flags while Pat Robertson was investing in television stations."

It is ironic that PAW founder Norman Lear aims to stifle the use of media by those who believe that traditional religion should have a role in public life, when he argued that freedom of expression should allow his own controversial shows to be aired.

"In truth, what was happening was that conservative preachers were taking on network television and the left didn't like it,"says William P. Hoar, senior editor of *Conservative Digest*. "Five of Lear's six polemical shows — heavy with left-wing or free-sex propaganda — had held the top ratings in one year. Best known was *All In The Family*'s Archie Bunker as an absurd stereotypical right-winger railing against what he called hebes, yids, coons, spics, dagos, chinks and fruits; there was his *Mary Hartman, Mary Hartman* show wallowing in such subjects as exhibitionism and masturbation; and the heroine of his *Maude* series was pumping Women's Lib, getting an abortion and pushing every available cause."

By the mid-70s more than half the U.S. population, some 120 million people, tuned in weekly to one of Lear's shows. Now he is worried about who is influencing the American public.

John Lofton, writing in *The Washington Times,* points out that PAW propagandists "said they oppose politicians citing Scripture to claim 'divine encouragement for ... candidates, platform planks and even congressional legislation.' When asked how this kind of thing, when done by religious conservatives now, differs from what liberal priests, rabbis and ministers did in the 1960s when these people quoted the Bible in support of civil rights, People For spokesmen called this a 'sticky issue.' They said that unlike 'extremists' whom they disapprove of (read: religious conservatives ...), civil rights activists in the 1960s quoted the Bible in nonsectarian, nondenominational and non-partisan ways."

Robertson laughs at their arguments. Said one of Pat's backers, "People for the American Way are being run over by a steamroller and they don't know how to stop it." A recent tactic used by PAW to discredit Robertson was to review hundreds of hours of *The 700 Club* to find video clips that attempt to paint him as a religious extremist. Their tape is entitled, "Pat Robertson: In His Own Words."

PAW admitted that their organization's project is designed to place him at the radical fringe of society. The video hits Robertson's views on Social Security, the banking system, education and the Constitution. For example, Robertson is shown criticizing the position of Supreme Court justices that constitutional rights would be the same in all 50 states. (The view that rights guaranteed by the Constitution apply to individual states, as well as nationally, has been the foundation of case law for many years).

The Washington Post wrote about an exchange of letters Robertson had with Lear. Robertson was quoted as referring to himself as "a prophet of God." When asked about it, he said, "Well, first of all, the People for the American Way have monitored every single broadcast I have done for at least the last five or six years. They have videotaped every word and they are spending large sums of money analyzing my statements to see if there are any possible fairness doctrine challenges in any of my statements."

Said Robertson, "I said on one of my broadcasts that, in the founding of America, 2.3 million Americans were Protestants, about 600,000 were Catholics and about 5,000 were Jewish. And the Founding Fathers of America were Christians. Well, I don't think a statement about history is considered a matter of public debate before the Congress of the United States today.

"Yet," says Pat, "Norman Lear and his group went to station KTOA-TV, which we were broadcasting on in Los Angeles and demanded a week of equal time. Once a station is forced to give up five half-hours of time for free, then it looks with a jaundiced eye on the broadcaster who is causing that problem.

"The next step," Robertson says, "would have been to have taken our program off the air in what is the second largest market in America. I knew if this type of attack kept up, we would have been taken off."

At the time Lear was reaching audiences of millions and Pat believed it seemed unfair "that a man with that kind of audience was trying to drive off the air a minister at 7 o'clock in the morning.

"So I wrote him in a sense to warn him that he wasn't just dealing with one more broadcaster in a rating war, that indeed he was dealing with a servant of God. When I used the term 'prophet of God,' I meant it as understood by most religious people: it means a spokesman. The liberal media seized on this as evidence of fanatical views but they just didn't understand the terms."

Especially alarming to his critics is the fact that Robertson describes answers to prayers that he believes are taking place during the program. For example, Robertson may say, "Someone right now is being healed of a sinus condition."

To Robertson, this is a biblically based spiritual "gift" that is available to Christians today.

It is known in theological circles as the "word of knowledge."

In a recent interview with the editors of *Christianity Today,* he was asked, "How much do you rely on it in your own decision making?"

Said Robertson, quoting the Bible, "In I Corinthians 12, the apostle Paul said the word of knowledge is for the church. The apostle Peter said that as each has received a gift, let him use it to benefit others (I Pet. 4:10).

"When someone is hurting," said Pat, "the Lord

sometimes shows another person what the problem is. I have had this experience when I'm counseling people. It helps me know what's going on in their lives so I can help them." He added, "But God doesn't give me words of knowledge in my own life."

To Robertson, the use of a biblical "gift" is quite natural and he has never tried to hide its occurrence. In his bestselling book _The Secret Kingdom_ he talks about the word of knowledge by saying, "Such a word quite simply reveals information the natural mind would not know, about a condition or a circumstance in which God is acting.

"For example," says Pat, "a woman in California was watching _The 700 Club_ while sitting in a great deal of discomfort from a broken ankle encased in a cast. She heard me say on the air, 'There's a woman in a cast. She has broken her ankle and God is healing her.'"

Says Robertson, "The woman immediately knew, in a burst of faith in her spirit, that those words had been spoken for her. She rose from the chair, removed the cast and, with increasing confidence, began to put weight on the broken foot and then to jump on it. The ankle bone had been healed."

What about faith healing?

Pat, on a national television program in March 1987 said, "If I ever find a faith healer in my organization I'll fire him. I don't believe in faith healers but I do believe in the power of God to heal."

Robertson makes no apology for the fact that he believes in prayer. He prays for small answers — and big ones. It was his prayer that God would turn back a hurricane that created hundreds of headlines.

In 1985, Pat prayed that Hurricane Gloria, heading straight for the shore near Virginia Beach, Virginia, would spare the area. He didn't pray in private but on television that the storm would spare Virginia Beach.

That is what happened.

Said Robertson later, "I believe if we ask God to do things, He will. The only difference between me and others is that I believe when I pray, I get answers."

But that was not the first time Robertson was bold enough to ask God to protect the area from a hurricane. In his book *Beyond Reason,* he says, "Back in the 1960s, Virginia Beach was threatened by a potentially devastating hurricane. Word reached us that a great killer hurricane with winds exceeding 150 miles per hour was heading directly into our area. We realized further that if the tower was blown over by the high winds, it would fall on our studio — and if the studio was destroyed, that would wipe out CBN."

Says Pat, "Our resources were so limited then that, short of a miracle, we would have a hard time recovering from such a disaster." In a public meeting, Robertson prayed out loud.

As he describes it, "faith rose within me and with authority in my voice" — he prayed that the hurricane would halt.

Hurricane Betsy stayed in the same area for about 24 hours, then turned back south where it had come from. Wrote Pat, "Skeptics may offer other explanations for these events. But I know it was God's power that spared this region and also our CBN tower."

He adds, "Certainly I don't believe that mere human beings possess the power to control the elements." But Robertson believes that by the proper exercise of divine gifts, Christians can perform greater works than most people dream.

As Robertson says, "being part of one of God's miracles doesn't always involve great notoriety or tremendous accolades. Nor are miracles intended to become some sort of 'proof' of faith."

The fact that Robertson talks to God is not a problem for most people. According to Gallup, about 90 percent of Americans say they do also (and that figure has remained constant for about four decades).

But what about God talking back?

In December 1986 another poll was released by Gallup that more than one in three Americans believe that God speaks specifically to them.

As it was reported, "Thirty-six percent of American

adults believe that God speaks to them directly. More than two-thirds of Americans believe that God has led or guided them in making decisions."

When asked about the survey and its significance to the Robertson issue, pollster George Gallup Jr. said, "The public is perhaps more open to a person saying he is receiving guidance from God than the press has indicated and not just in terms of Pat's statements about hurricanes and so forth but also in a broad sense."

Since a great number of Americans have felt the same spiritual guidance, Gallup says, "the public understands when a leader says God has spoken to him or guided him to take a specific course of action. It strikes a responsive chord, not just in terms of Pat Robertson but in any area of life — business, cultural, athletic," he said. "The public doesn't reject that concept; that's what these figures say to me basically."

The poll found that 94 percent of adult Americans believe in God or some universal spirit and that 84 percent believe "God is a heavenly father who watches over us and can be reached by our prayers."

When asked if God had ever led or guided them in making a decision, 69 percent answered, "Yes."

The poll revealed additional information of possible significance to Robertson. It found that 31 percent of adult Americans identify themselves as born-again, or evangelical Christians. (Thirty-seven percent of Republicans surveyed identified themselves as evangelicals, compared to 33 percent of Democrats and 26 percent of independents).

Today, Pat Robertson stands on center stage of the conservative, evangelical, charismatic world. The spotlight is often in the hands of media but the audience is made up of millions of people from all races, socio-economic backgrounds and faiths. They identify with him, not as a radical evangelist but as a friend who has come into their homes. He has reasoned with them. Laughed with them. Informed them. His staff has counseled with them.

As Roger Adams, a salesman in Los Angeles told

me, "When I was a boy in school, we used to pledge allegiance to the flag, saying, 'One nation, under God.' I believe Pat Robertson can make that pledge come true."

12

His Father's Son

At a Presidential Inauguration, America heard these words: "I have a profound reverence for the Christian religion and a thorough conviction that sound morals, religious liberty and a just sense of religious responsibility are essentially connected with all true and lasting happiness."

They were spoken by a noted member of Pat's family tree, U.S. President William Henry Harrison, as he took the oath of office March 4, 1841.

Today, in every community in America, there is a vocal group of people who would like those words to be commonplace at every level of government.

The one individual who is being asked to be the "point man" for the concerns of conservative Christians is Pat Robertson.

"It isn't worth debating whether they sought him or he sought them," said one observer. "The point is, their views are a mirror image."

Robertson's position on major issues is perhaps better known by more Americans than any public figure. Not even the president of the United States can match Robertson's record. For nearly two decades Pat has spent at least 30 minutes a day speaking on national television to upwards of 4.5 million daily viewers. Contrary to those who dismiss him lightly, he has been speaking directly to major national and international issues.

Besides television, he has used the printed page to duplicate his words to additional millions.

What does he stand for? Here's just a sample, from

the newsletter he published for several years, *Pat Robertson's Perspective:*

• He supports the sale of arms to anti-communist
countries.

• He believes that both government and individuals
should operate on a bare minimum of credit.

• He opposes mixing the institutional church and
government.

• He opposes a national health insurance plan.

• He wants the United States to undertake a major
military buildup against Russia.

• He is against any homosexual rights legislation.

• He supports the use of nuclear power.

• He backs Israel strongly.

• He does not believe Israel should give up any oc-
cupied land.

• He supports a balanced budget.

• He is a strong advocate of private education.

• He favors lower government taxation.

• He advocates less governmental intervention in
state, local, business and private affairs.

• He favors the deregulation of industry.

In print and on television it is almost impossible to
find an issue he has not addressed. He not only discusses
topics with deep personal understanding and analysis —
he takes a stand.

A regular CBN viewer from Chicago said, "I've
learned more about world events watching Pat than I ever
imagined. He makes it so clear and down to earth."

Robertson is an individualist and a creative thinker
but he has surrounded himself with a cadre of conservative intellectuals, both in the CBN University graduate
school of Public Policy and his close circle of advisors.
Their input has only enlarged Pat's ready storehouse of
information.

What are CBNU's students being taught? Here's a
sample from the Public Policy course offerings: Crime
and Punishment, Restitution and Redemption, Inalienable
Rights and Liberties, Energy and Geopolitics, War and
Peace: Judgment unto Righteousness, Political Involve-

ment, Biblical Principles of Law and Welfare: God, Man, Love and Community.

The university is certainly not a propaganda tool for Robertson's views. In the February 1987 issue of the 20-page student newspaper *The Standard,* the entire issue dealt with political and social issues. Articles were titled "Defending America," "The Bible and the Bomb," "The Specter of Communism," "The Morality of SDI," and "Avoiding Holocaust in the Nuclear Age."

Nowhere could I find the name of Robertson in the publication. Not even a quote. On television and on the platform, however, Robertson is extremely comfortable in dealing with issues. That should come as no surprise. He was raised in an atmosphere where the dinner conversation would range from international tariffs to county politics. As the son of a U.S. senator, Pat learned much at his father's knee. He has not forgotten it. Said one old-timer in Lexington, "You can close your eyes and think you are listening to the speeches of A. Willis Robertson."

Political observer Garrett Epps in *The Washington Post.* said, "Like his father, Pat holds an old-fashioned Southern view of the Constitution. Like his father, he is highly conservative on social issues, fiercely anti-communist and pro-military and critical of deficit spending and welfare programs."

He added, "And like his father, he sees nothing wrong with invoking the Bible and religious values in political debate."

It is refreshing to examine Robertson's position on specific issues, knowing the elements of his life that have forged his positions. In his words you can feel the influences of his political father, his deeply religious mother, his worldly wise social and cultural understanding, his business savvy, his education with degrees in history, law and biblical studies, his experience in the ghetto — and with God.

Let's look at the issues.

Where is Robertson coming from regarding the conflict between church and state? In a recent interview with *Southern Partisan,* Pat said, "I think the popular conception of the separation of church and state is one of the great fictions that has been foisted upon us by those who do not like religion. I am a firm believer that the church — as an institution — should not be trying to manipulate government — as an institution.

"Certainly," said Robertson, "the Constitution was meant to prevent government from interfering with worship. This is what should be separate but there is nothing in any of our Constitutional writings, our history or our experience to indicate that we should separate morality from government or that moral, godly people should be taken away from the government. As a matter of fact," he added, "the Constitution specifically states that there shall be no religious test for any office or position of trust under the Constitution."

To Robertson, the issue is liberty and the free exercise of freedom, religious or otherwise.

As he told *Conservative Digest,* "Religious people, whether Christians or Jews, appreciate the contribution religious liberty has made to our society over the past two hundred years. They understand the value of carefully defining the sphere of governmental authority and the need continually to keep the hearts and minds — the beliefs and thoughts — of the citizenry beyond the jurisdiction of government."

He added this significant point: "Similarly, non-religious people enjoy the assurance that government cannot, as the 1786 Virginia Statute for Religious Freedom put it, '... diminish, enlarge or affect their civil capacities' based on religious opinion or belief."

Robertson's tolerance and respect for those holding opposing positions comes as a surprise for many of his critics. Not all of Robertson's views are carbon copies of today's conservatives. Take the issue of the Supreme Court: "A decision of the Supreme Court is not the supreme law of the land, because the Constitution provides what is the supreme law of the land."

No, that is not Pat speaking but his father, A. Willis Robertson, addressing the United States Senate on March 3, 1960.

As Garrett Epps points out, "Willis Robertson's view of the Constitution was common among Southern politicians at the time: The school integration decisions of the United States Supreme Court, he argued, could legally be overturned by acts of Congress.

"If those words sound familiar," said Epps, "consider these remarks made by Pat Robertson to a gathering of editors at *The Washington Post* in 1986: 'A Supreme Court ruling is not the law of the United States. The law of the United States is the Constitution, treaties made in accordance with the Constitution and laws duly enacted by Congress and signed by the president.' "

Many who read Pat's statement thought they were hearing a radical new position. It was a concept he had been raised on and thoroughly understood.

What about education? Robertson has strong opinions concerning schools, prayer in the classroom, book banning and secular humanism.

"There is a conscious, deliberate attempt to move the majority of students in America's schools away from our traditional family, moral and religious values and move them into an amoral, secular, internationalist, social mode," said Robertson at a recent speaking engagement in Midland, Michigan.

More and more he is speaking out on the issue of how he believes a godless attitude has resulted in a moral vacuum in our educational system. He wants prayer returned to the schools.

Robertson said recently, "For the sake of our children we must bring God back to the classroom ... 94 percent of all Americans believe in God. Only 6 percent are atheists. I do not believe that the 94 percent of us who believe in God have any duty whatsoever to dismantle our entire public affirmation of faith in God."

Again, Pat is preaching his father's message to a new generation. "Willis Robertson in 1962 passionately denounced the United States Supreme Court decision that outlawed official prayer in the public schools," said Garrett Epps in *The Washington Post*. "In words that are echoed today by Pat, Willis argued that the court had misunderstood the First Amendment: 'Clearly the words "establishment of religion" in the First Amendment were intended to mean the establishment of a particular denomination — Methodist, Baptist or Catholic — as the national religion.

" 'And clearly the 14th Amendment was not intended to apply the establishment clause of the First Amendment to the states.' If the courts continue to apply the First Amendment to religious affairs of the states, said the senator from Virginia, they would 'undoubtedly sweep us down the broad and easy highway of secularism.' "

Now Pat is applying the same logic to a new set of circumstances. Today the fight concerns "secular humanism" and Robertson is not only leading the parade, he's put on his old boxing gloves.

In March 1987 a court ruling in Alabama was a major decision for those who want to rid the public schools of texts which are devoid of moral values. As reported in *Time,* "The First Amendment bans any governmental 'establishment of religion.' So, to avoid objections from school boards, textbook publishers have often purged mention of the religious underpinnings of events like Thanksgiving or of moral values involving such matters as teenage sex and divorce."

What resulted, said concerned Christian parents, was a creed of its own — secular humanism. In a bold decision U.S. District Judge W. Brevard Hand banned 45 textbooks from Alabama public schools because they promote, unconstitutionally, "the religion of secular humanism."

Said *Time,* "His ruling ... prompted hosannas from the religious right. 'Humanism will no longer be guaranteed a preferred position in American education,' exulted Robert Skolrood, executive director of the National Legal Foundation, a group established by television evangelist Pat Robertson that helped represent the plaintiff parents and teachers." Said Skolrood, "Humanism and its hidden agenda are now out of the closet."

Writing in *USA Today* from a Virginia Beach dateline, Skolrood explained, "The Supreme Court has held that there must be strict neutrality and equal treatment of all religions. The United States District Court in Mobile found humanism to be a religion. Is it not fair to ask it to abide by the same rules as other religions? To answer to the contrary is to advocate preferred treatment of one religion over another; it's hardly fair," said Skolrood, "to allow one religion to exclusively indoctrinate our children."

Robertson naturally was overjoyed with the stunning victory his National Legal Foundation had won. Earlier, in the fall of 1981, he had written, "Today, under the assault of secular humanism, a new rule of law is emerging. No longer do judges seek to make decisions based on the Bible, the Constitution, natural law or historic precedent.

"Instead they impose as a rule of law whatever seems sociologically expedient or whatever reflects the prevailing sentiment of the ruling humanistic elite. As one justice declared arrogantly, 'The Constitution is whatever we say it is.'" Said Pat, "We have ceased to be a government of law and have become a government of men."

Pat has said, "Our children and grandchildren are our greatest national treasure. We owe them a secure and loving family environment. We owe them strong homes and a mother and father who care for them, spend time with them and truly love them. We owe them a future filled with excitement and hope — not a legacy of moral and economic bankruptcy."

On the topic of fiscal policy, Robertson has an amazing understanding. In a debate or on a panel of "experts," audiences, especially secular ones, are surprised with his expertise.

Listen to what he wrote in the September 1981 issue of *Perspective:* "Consider the plight of business. As the economy slows down they must borrow just to keep up with inflation. The bond market is not a realistic alternative in today's economy, so there is a rush for short-term credit despite merciless interest.

"If the economy does not expand rapidly, these businesses must borrow even more just to pay their interest.

As exponential compounding continues, weaker businesses are either forced to liquidate or to spend all of their creative energies as the servants of their lenders.

"Estimates of debt vary," said Pat, "but an illustrative working estimate would be $5 trillion of private and public debt in the United States and an equal amount overseas. The actual amount of money supply is approximately one-tenth of the total amount of debt outstanding. The United States M-1 figures are roughly $430 billion.

"In other words," Robertson states, "because of the exponential growth of worldwide debt, it appears that there is only enough money in the world to pay interest on all debt at a 10 percent rate."

Then he gave what he called "a simple illustration" to underscore the point.

Said Pat, "If you borrow $100 from a bank at 6 percent interest and you put the money in a checking account, the money supply increases by $100, your debt is $100 and your annual interest payment is $6. If you pay no interest on the loan for fifty years but compound it, at the end of fifty years your debt will be $1,737.75, your interest payments will be $104.26 and your share of the money supply will still be $100. If additional credit is made available under the same conditions, the money supply will expand accordingly but never in adequate amounts to service the compound interest on debt."

Robertson's analysis continued, leading to the conclusion that because of the compounding of interest, a money trap is formed from which there is no possible escape.

"Then debt is eliminated by bankruptcy, debt repudiation, hyperinflation, dictatorial slavery or a brand new money system," he said.

His bottom line? Get your financial house in order. That's his advice for both nations and individuals.

As he told a *Time* reporter, "The Bible says very cogently, 'Do not forsake wisdom.' Deficit spending is neither left wing or right wing; it is just stupid. Balanced budgets make sense ... We are stealing the patrimony from our future generations."

On international issues, Robertson has a great deal of first-hand experience. CBN operates in over 70 nations and Pat has personally met with heads of states of dozens of nations.

Regarding the East-West struggle, he said recently, "I think that Soviet Russia is destined to fall and I don't think the United States has to go to war with them to see that happen. It will continue to lose because the system violates basic human nature."

What about the nuclear arms race with the Soviets? Answering a reporter's question, he said, "Ideally, in the Bible Jesus said, 'Resist not evil.' You can certainly read pacifism into the words that Jesus said. Conversely, I'm from the area where Patrick Henry stood up and said, 'Is life so dear or peace so sweet to be purchased at the price of chains and slavery?' "

Says Robertson, "The Bible tells us that we are to lift the yoke of oppression and in today's world we see the yoke of oppression has come down on about a billion people. There's no question that if the communists took charge of this nation, for example, I'd end up in a concentration camp.

"The reality of it," says Pat, "is that the Soviets ... want to control the world. They're doing it step by step. They have built the most awesome nuclear arsenal that has ever been known to man."

Robertson has made it clear that he wants peace "and it looks as if a nuclear standoff in the last thirty years is the best way of getting it."

In his view, if the United States happened to be the only nuclear power in the world, "I'd say get rid of every nuclear bomb that had ever been made." But, knowing the intentions of the Soviets, he believes that operating from a position of strength is the only way to stabilize the situation.

Regarding Central America, his role in Nicaragua has been a subject of considerable interest. "I favor the Contras and I favor the cause of freedom any place in the world against communist aggression," he told *Charisma* magazine. "I think Daniel Ortega has fastened a repressive communist regime on the people of Nicaragua. There have been atrocities against the Mesquito Indians. There have been atrocities against members of the civilian population and there has been systematic persecution of churches.

"I have facilitated the shipment of medicine and food to needy refugees in Honduras, Costa Rica and Guatemala," said Robertson. "We are in the process of paying $2 million for the transport of $20 million of goods for distribution to refugees in Guatemala. It's all humanitarian aid and I'm proud of it."

Whatever the issue, however, he is quick to see the spiritual significance. Says Pat, "Our leaders must understand the relationship between righteousness and the prosperity or ultimate decline of our nation. Christians, on the other hand, must understand that neither Republicans nor Democrats, liberals nor conservatives, have any corner on the Kingdom of God."

Although Robertson can be rigid on his personal beliefs, he is a realist when it comes to accommodating a variety of opinions. When asked about the topic of compromise by *Charisma* magazine, he said, "I think the only way people can accomplish anything politically in a pluralistic society as large as the United States of America is through coalitions and some degree of compromise. The government and its officials must never lie to the people or steal or cheat — in short they must conduct themselves morally. In terms of procedures or various initiatives and the allocations of funds — these things are all matters of political compromise ... "

Regarding the ERA and the role of women in society, Dede Robertson offered an opinion recently. "I don't think the women's movement ever spoke to the majority of women. The ERA was too broad a statement. I believe in equal pay for equal work and I encourage women to be more active. Politics is a wide open field for women to get into."

Then she smiled and added, "Let the husband put food on the table and women run for office."

When Pat was asked about involvement in government, he said, "I believe that in our country we have a unique opportunity to render to Caesar intelligent citizenship. I perceive in our country an all-out assault on a number of Christian values. There is an assault on the family, there's an assault on the beliefs that we have held in the Bible and the scriptural concept of man."

Robertson looks at man as "being made in God's image and endowed with certain inalienable rights because of a creator." However, he notes, if "we regard man as the sum total of behavior patterns" and "having no rights in his self but taking his rights from the government, he is set up for every kind of repressive type of system that others want to devise and put him under."

Robertson added, "When you begin widespread deficit spending, you eliminate the old capitalist Puritan ethic which is that you should save and be frugal."

Then, he observes, you soon adopt the philosophy that says, "I'm going to seize the day, whatever pleasure I can take, because values are so transitory and therefore I'd better overspend now because my store of economic value is being taken away from me by a profligate government." Robertson believes that kind of thinking has an undermining effect on the moral fabric of the nation.

"I think that Christians as citizens in a free society should get involved in government and try to reverse some of these changes," he said.

But for Robertson, his major theme is the American society and what can be done to bring a moral revolution to the nation.

He shared with his supporters a scenario of what he sees happening in this country. It reveals the deep concern he has for the nation: "A significant minority, then a majority of the people in a society begin to throw off the restraints of history — then the restraints of written law — then accepted standards of morality — then established religion — finally God himself.

"As the rebellion gains momentum, the participants grow bolder. What was once considered shameful and unlawful begins to be practiced openly, then militantly. As each societal taboo falls, another comes under attack, established institutions crumble. What begins as a cry for 'freedom of expression' soon turns into an all-out war against the rights of the advocates of traditional morality," he said.

He continued, "The thing spreads like a disease. Honor, decency, honesty, self-control, sexual restraint, family values and sacrifice are replaced by gluttony, sensuality, bizarre sex, cruelty, dishonesty, fraud, waste, debauched currency, rampant inflation, delinquency, drunkenness and drug-induced euphoria. Those who represent traditional morality are hated, then reviled, then diminished in influence and finally persecuted as enemies."

The picture Robertson paints is not a pretty one. The people, he says, "then seek out a deity which will both permit and personify their basest desires. At Babel it was a tower; in ancient Mediterranean cultures it was a god or goddess of sex; at Mt. Sinai it was a golden calf; in Rome it was an insane emperor; in France it was the goddess of reason; in Germany it was Adolf Hitler and the Nazi party; in the United States it is central government under the religion of secular humanism."

He adds, "No society under the grip of the antichristian spirit has ever survived. With it comes a period of lawlessness and virtual anarchy. Then an economic collapse followed by a reign of terror. Then a strong man dictator who plunders the society for his own personal aggrandizement. Then wars to fulfill the leader's insane dream of empire. Then defeat and collapse."

Then, he warns, "Consider what has been happening in the United States." He talks about organized crime being the largest industry in America — narcotics, prostitution, gambling, pornography and racketeering.

Robertson describes a nation mired in crime and drug abuse. He says they are only part of the story: "Consider the sexual revolution. Public standards regarding nudity, fornication, adultery, homosexuality, incest, child molestation and sadomasochism have either crumbled or are under fierce attack."

He then decries sex education without moral standards, pornography that has crept into major motion pictures, plus homosexuality and abortion.

"As an accommodation to their views, the Supreme Court of the United States has ruled that the thing conceived as the result of sexual relations between two human beings is not itself a human being and therefore may be destroyed prior to birth. It is an embryo, a fetus or the 'product of conception' but *not* a human baby," he said.

What is the answer? Pat says, "At the core of a self-governing free society there must be self-restraint on the part of the people. This self-restraint springs from the belief that there is a God who is the ultimate authority, who will one day reward or punish men for their conduct on earth. No democratic society can endure without self-restraint based on moral absolutes."

To dedicated Christians in America, Pat believes morality is the primary concern: "Their hopes, their dreams, their economics and their politics center around their faith in God." Says Robertson, "To the Jews, the Holocaust was not a peripheral issue. It was life and death. To the blacks, freedom from oppression and equality of opportunity was not an optional extra. To them it made up their entire political agenda."

Pat believes that items on the conservative agenda — "supply-side economics, strong defense, tax cuts, balanced budgets, the deregulation of industry, sound currency — are important. What good are any of them" he asks, if the nation destroys itself?

"Americans must wake up to what is happening," he says as he calls on people to pray. He says, "There must be education in our heritage, our laws and the way our system functions. Christians must stand in defense of freedom. They must resist the antichristian spirit in the public arena, in the courts and in the polls."

Yes, in the polls. He believes the scenario that would destroy this nation does not have to occur. He does not believe it is too late to turn the nation around.

Pat has made a commitment to lead the way.

The enthusiasm for a Robertson candidacy is building fast. At a March 1987 rally in Columbia, South Carolina, about 1,000 Robertson supporters jammed the Radisson Hotel.

State Senator John Courson, Republican national committeeman, said he was "stunned" by the size of the crowd. "I couldn't believe what I saw when I walked in here," he said.

But I certainly could.

Talking with Robertson at his home during CBN's 25th Anniversary celebration, he told me, "Everywhere I go, people are telling me to 'Go for it. Go for it.' "

He had that same sparkle in his eye as the day he looked into the camera and said, "Welcome to the Christian Broadcasting Network."

I could not help but wonder.

What will we be celebrating next?